the new
Learning About Sex

a series for
the Christian family

5

ages
14–young adult

Love
Sex
and God

Bill Ameiss and Jane Graver

For Discussion or Individual Use

CONCORDIA PUBLISHING HOUSE · SAINT LOUIS

Acknowledgments

We wish to thank the following for their special contributions to the Learning About Sex Series:

Frederick J. Hofmeister, M.D., FACOG, Wauwatosa, Wisconsin, served as medical adviser for the series. Micheal J. Chehval, M.D., urologist and Chief of Staff at St. John's Mercy Medical Center, St. Louis, Missouri, provided an additional medical review.

Rev. Ronald W. Brusius, secretary of family life education, Board for Parish Services of the LCMS, served as chief subject matter consultant.

Kathryn Krieger and Rodney Rathmann, Day-Midweek Department, CPH, contributed special expertise in the review and editing of manuscripts.

The following provided invaluable help in their areas of expertise: Darlene Armbruster, board member, National Lutheran Parent-Teacher League; Betty Brusius, executive director, National Lutheran Parent-Teacher League; Margaret Gaulke, elementary school guidance counselor; Priscilla Henkelman, early childhood specialist; Rev. Lee Hovel, youth specialist; Robert G. Miles, Lutheran Child and Family Service of Michigan; Margaret Noettl, family life specialist; and Bonnie Schlechte, lecturer on teen sexuality.

Book 5 of the Learning about Sex series

The titles in the series:

Contents

Editor's Foreword

This book is one of a series of six designed to help parents communicate Christian values to their children in the area of sexuality. A seventh book, *Human Sexuality: A Christian Perspective*, deals with the spiritual, emotional, and physical aspects of the God-given gift of sexuality. Both the single adult and the married will profit from the practical, biblically-oriented content of this last book in the series.

Love, Sex, and God is the fifth book in the series. It is written especially for youth ages 14 and older—and, of course, for the parents, teachers, and other significant grownups who may want to discuss the book with them.

Like its predecessor, the new Learning about Sex series provides information about the social-psychological and physiological aspects of human sexuality. But more: it does so from a distinctively Christian point of view, in the context of our relationship to the God who created us and redeemed us in Jesus Christ.

The series presents sex as another good gift from God which is to be used responsibly.

Each book in the series is graded—in vocabulary and in the amount of information it provides. It answers the questions that persons at each age level typically ask.

Because children vary widely in their growth rates and interest levels, parents and other concerned adults will want to preview each book in the series, directing the child to the next graded book when he or she is ready for it.

In addition to reading each book, you can use them as starting points for casual conversation and when answering other questions a child might have.

This book can also be used as a mini-unit or as part of another course of study in a Christian school setting. (Correlated video and study resources are available for both curricular and home use.)

Whenever the book is used in a class setting, it is important to let the parents know beforehand, since they have the prime responsibility for the sex education of their children.

While parents will appreciate the help of the school, they will want to know what is being taught. As the Christian home and the Christian school work together, Christian values in sex education can be more effectively strengthened.

Rev. Earl H. Gaulke, Ph.D., D.D.

Introduction

What do other people really think of me?

Am I normal?

How can I let him know I like him a lot?

How can I get to know her better?

How can I tell if I'm really in love?

What if I'm in trouble?

Where should I go for help?

These are not unusual questions. The purpose of this book is to explore these and a whole range of related questions and subjects. We'll draw on the questions, struggles, and experiences of many young people as they too have faced the responsibilities of the upper-teen years. We'll try to help you use their questions and experiences together with reliable physiological information, as you work through what it means to be a sexual, Christian human being.

The Bible gives us the basis and the standards for our life with God, our relationship with others, and our attitudes about our own sexuality.

So it is, that through the upper-teen years and all through life, the encouraging thing is that God really is "Lord of Life and Lord of Me."

Chapter 1

Sex and Sexuality

SEX IS ... SEXUALITY IS

In your opinion, which of the following is the best definition of sex? the second-best? the third-best?

- a physical desire
- being male or female
- a gift of God
- an embarrassing subject
- sexual intercourse

The word *sex*, strictly speaking, is the quality of being male or female, depending on the physical makeup of the individual.

Comparisons are often tricky, but one way might be to compare sex to a new car.

A new car has wheels, bolts, gears—all the parts that are necessary for a car to run.

A person has male or female hormones, male or female sexual organs—all the parts that are necessary to function as a man or a woman.

A new car is good. When you have one, you're proud of it.

Your sex is good. It is a gift from God, something to be proud of.

In order to say and appreciate what your sex adds to your whole life and character, you usually use the word *sexuality*.

Let's take the comparison a step further:

A new car doesn't mean much if it just sits in the driveway. It's how you use it and take care of it that counts.

Your sexuality includes your sex organs—as well as the way you think and feel about them and use them. It takes into account everything you are as male and female.

Like anything else, cars and sex can be used responsibly—or they can be abused ... or they can be misused. If we drive our cars or use our sex to hurt others, God may forgive us, but His forgiveness does not take away the consequences of our actions. The run-over pedestrian is still dead; the unmarried pregnant girl is still pregnant.

Driving recklessly may look like fun, but it isn't in the long run. Damages and injuries are hardly fun.

Eight-year-old Jason might think he's driving when Dad lets him make believe he's steering the car. But driving is a lot harder—and a lot more interesting—than steering.

Sexual irresponsibility may look like fun, but it isn't in the long run. Guilt and broken relationships for ourselves and others are hardly fun.

People who just think of sex (body only) instead of sexuality (all of you—body and spirit) miss the greatest gift: a deeply satisfying relationship with another human being.

Sexuality in the Media

What attitudes about sex do you see reflected in
- the magazines you read (or look at)?
- the movie you saw most recently?
- your favorite TV show?
- the songs you listen to?
- the images you see on some Internet sites?

Do these show responsible, sexual persons, who, though imperfect and vulnerable, do have a set of values—or do they picture glamorous figures who live in a world of fantasy? Does the story tell of trust, communication, and caring between two loving people—or does it imply that physical attraction is all there is?

Many ads, movies, TV shows, etc., seem to be written for the lowest level of maturity and intelligence. If we constantly fill our minds with words and pictures that show sex as an aggressive and impersonal act, we may find it hard to maintain our own moral values and to develop lasting, loving relationships.

On the other hand, we can learn from movies, books, and other media that honestly describe a growing relationship between two real people, even if those people act in ways we might disagree with. We can learn from both the good and the bad choices of others.

Even when a book or a movie appears to reflect real life with reasonable honesty, you may wonder whether things would really turn out the way they do in the story. Here's a plot you may have seen recently: Shortly after the hero and heroine meet and fall in love, they hop into bed. There are no doubts, no second thoughts, and no worries about unwelcome consequences. Sexual intercourse appears to be a normal, expected part of dating.

- What movies or TV shows have you seen that imply that it's okay because everybody does it?
- What effect might this subtle message have on a person who has not thought through his or her own values?
- Have you ever heard the statement, "Sex sells"? Does it help to explain why bedroom scenes are found in so many books, TV shows, and movies? What about advertisements that imply that a given product will make you sexier ... more attractive?

Masculinity and Femininity

Which of the following phrases describe a man? Which describe a woman? Which could describe both?

is a good cook	is competitive
is sensitive to others' feelings	is aggressive
is athletic	is independent
is courageous	is a leader
cries easily	cries when very sad
can change a tire	can clean, sew, do laundry
uses power tools	can speak and write well
does minor repairs	likes touching, tenderness
likes pretty things	

Tradition vs. Change

The way you answer the above will depend mostly on what you have become accustomed to. In the past, people had very definite ideas on roles for men and women. In our culture, men were expected to be the leaders at home and in society. They were expected to be wise, strong, and brave at all times—never showing emotion, never needing help. It was assumed that women's lives were centered on their homes; they were protected, guided, and supported by their men.

The big advantage of the traditional system was that everyone knew exactly what was expected of him or her. Life may have been dull sometimes, but at least you knew what was expected of you.

In today's world, changes have taken place. You can decide how you will act as a male or a female. For instance, Amy loves to cook. She looks forward to making a home for her husband and children some day. But Juana loves to work with electronics. Whenever she daydreams about the future, she imagines a career as an engineer.

On the other hand, Manuel enjoys being with Sara, who shares his interests—art, music, and serious conversation. The first time Sara beat Manuel in tennis, it bothered him; then he realized he doesn't have to be tops at any sport to prove he is a man. He used to pretend to be tough and unemotional. Now Sara encourages him to show his real feelings. She admires him for his honesty.

Although these young people are very different from one another, all of them are normal. As long as they recognize that they do have choices, they will not be trapped by inflexible ideas of what male or female should be. They can be free to be honest with themselves, to stay in touch with their own feelings about manhood or womanhood. Each person can choose his or her own version of what it means to be a man or a woman.

Beginnings of Sexuality

You began to be a man or a woman at the instant of conception. At your birth your parents joyfully said, "It's a boy!" or "It's a girl!" From that moment on, everyone treated you as a boy or as a girl. By the age of two you were watching others of your sex very carefully so you could imitate their walk, mannerisms, or speech. Your gender (being male or female) is so firmly a part of you that nothing can shake your deep knowledge of who you are.

Statistics show that boys are more likely to be good at math, more physically aggressive, and more independent than girls. Girls are more likely to be good at reading, more verbally aggressive, and more skilled at developing relationships. Are the sexes born with all these differences, or do we learn them from the way we are treated by others? Most scientists believe that it's a combination of these two factors.

Choose Your Own Roles

It's not easy to sort out today's conflicting definitions of masculinity and femininity.

Men hear these conflicting statements today:

"Only cowards back off from a fight."
"Peace is sometimes more important than winning."
"Never show weakness. Above all, *never* cry."
"A healthy male is someone who freely expresses his feelings and emotions."
"It's unmanly to cook, clean, or take care of children. That's women's work."
There is no "woman's work."

Women hear these conflicting statements today:

"You must have a career to fulfill yourself."
"It is your duty to stay home and care for your children."
"Be assertive and competitive. Men will take advantage of you if you let them."
"Although we are equal to men, we are different. Each sex has its strengths and weaknesses."
"The man in your life, your father or your husband, will take care of you."
"Every woman needs to know how to take care of herself."

As you sort through statements like these, take a hard look at the ones that pretend that all men or all women are alike. If you study the people around you, you will probably discover that there are at least as many differences between any two men or any two women as there are between men and women as groups.

Your masculinity or your femininity is an unshakable part of every cell in your body. When you are sure of something, you no longer have to prove it. You are free to be yourself.

Chapter 2

The Male and the Female Sexual Systems

Girls ask:

Why am I developing slower than my girlfriends?

How can a penis fit in a vagina?

Am I supposed to be menstruating at the same time every month?

Guys ask:

Is it normal to have wet dreams?

How come I get an erection when I'm not thinking about sex?

Why aren't penises all the same size?

Many young people know a lot about sex, but often their information has some half-truths and myths mixed in. This chapter will give a quick review of the facts you already know, with special attention to common questions asked by teens.

The Male Sexual System

For from Him and through Him and to Him are all things.
Romans 11:36

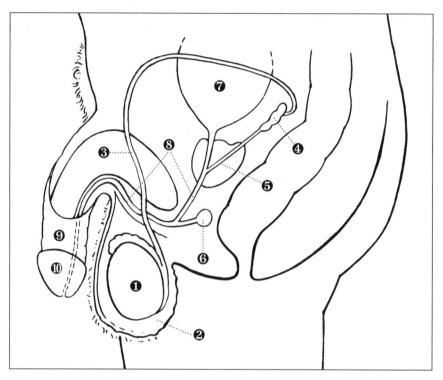

The male reproductive organs:

1. Testicles
2. Scrotum
3. Vas Deferens
4. Seminal Vesicles
5. Prostate Gland
6. Cowper's Glands
7. Bladder
8. Urethra
9. Penis
10. Glans

The Testicles

The **testicles** are roundish glands that hang just behind the penis in a pouch called the **scrotum.** Why is the left testicle lower (and sometimes larger) than the right one? Is this a mistake in God's creation? No—it's really a miracle of design, for it keeps the testicles from getting hurt as your legs come together.

Consider, too, God's wisdom in putting the testicles in the scrotum—*outside* the rest of the body. In this way the testicles are able to maintain the temperature they need—about 4° lower than the rest of the body. In cold weather the muscles of the scrotum contract to bring the testicles close to the body. In warm weather the muscles relax to lower the testicles away from the body. In this way the testicles are always kept near the proper temperature.

A boy's testicles are inside his body until a few weeks before he is born. Then the testicles descend into the scrotum. In about 3% of boy baby births, one or both testicles do not come out into the scrotum. Although a doctor's help is needed to correct this condition, these boys are usually normal in every other way.

The testicles produce **sperm,** tiny cells that are needed for reproduction. From **puberty** into old age, these amazing glands make millions of sperm a day. Sperm can be seen only through a microscope; one drop of fluid can contain 120 million of them. They look like tadpoles with skinny, active tails.

Another important job of the testicles is to produce **testosterone,** a **hormone** or chemical that controls the development of male sex characteristics—like a beard and lower voice. During puberty, boys notice that the testicles and **penis** grow and become darker in color; hair grows in the **pubic** area and later on the body and face; the voice deepens; and muscles and bones grow very rapidly. Suddenly boys are interested in girls in a new and exciting way.

The Sperm Storage and Transportation System

After sperm are produced in tiny tubes inside the testicles, they move to larger tubes, where they mature. Then they travel through another tube (the **vas deferens)** to the **seminal vesicles,** which are two pouches just behind the **bladder.** Next to the seminal vesicles is an active little gland, the **prostate.** It constantly manufactures a fluid that mixes with fluids from other glands to make **semen.**

Semen is the white, sticky fluid in which sperm leave the penis. Only 1–3 teaspoons of semen leave the body at any one time.

The Penis

The penis hangs in front of the testicles. Like the testicles, the penis is very sensitive to contact. The **glans,** the end of the penis, is especially sensitive. It is covered with a loose elastic skin, the **foreskin.**

Many doctors recommend **circumcision** (removing the foreskin) to prevent dirt or urine from collecting under the foreskin and thus causing infection. Usually this simple operation is done soon after birth, but it can be done at any age. Circumcision does not affect a male's ability to give or receive sexual pleasure.

Erections

When a man is sexually aroused, the soft, limp tissue of his penis becomes **erect** and larger—hard enough to stand away from the body. Even though there is a difference in the size and shape of penises, there is little difference in the sexual satisfaction for either man or woman.

The inside of a penis is a lot like a sponge. During an erection extra blood rushes into the penis. Valves close to hold this blood under pressure.

Erections can happen at any age, but they seem to happen more often during **adolescence.** They can be caused by sexual feelings and daydreams, but they also occur because of tight clothing, pressure from a full bladder—or even for no apparent reason. Although it can be very embarrassing when it happens in public, it is usually not very noticeable to other people.

Ejaculation

If the stimulation that causes an erection is continued, semen moves into the **urethra** tube. Strong muscles move it along until it squirts or oozes from the penis. This **ejaculation,** or squirting out of semen, goes along with intense feelings of pleasure, called an **orgasm.** Although semen and urine both leave the body through the urethra, they cannot pass through the penis at the same time. Special muscles close off the bladder when the penis is erect.

When the seminal vesicles are full, ejaculation may take place during sleep. This is called a **nocturnal emission,** or a **wet dream** because of the sex dream that may happen during the ejaculation.

Sometimes young men feel guilt or embarrassment about nocturnal emissions. Yet they are completely natural. They are part of God's design for relieving sexual tensions and releasing surplus semen.

The Female Sexual System

For from Him and through Him and to Him are all things.
Romans 11:36

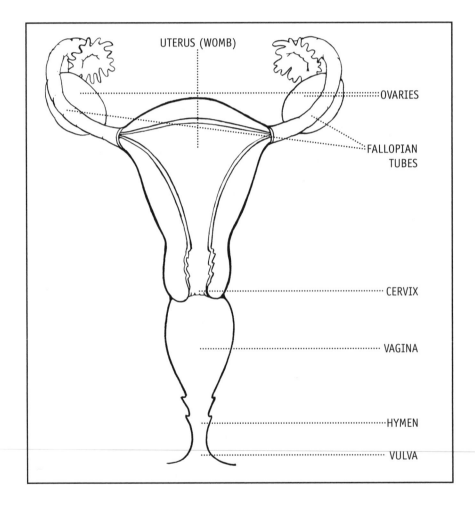

UTERUS (WOMB)

OVARIES

FALLOPIAN TUBES

CERVIX

VAGINA

HYMEN

VULVA

The Internal Sexual Organs

Deep inside the female body is a pair of **ovaries.** They contain thousands of undeveloped egg cells. When a girl is somewhere between the ages of 9 and 16, her ovaries begin to produce **estrogen,** the female **hormone** that controls many changes in her body.

During the next few years her breasts develop and her hips broaden. Her height and weight increase rapidly. And her **sex organs** grow. Hair appears under her arms and in her pubic area. As **menstruation** begins, she may also notice a clear whitish discharge from her **vagina.**

At **puberty** the egg cells in the ovaries begin to ripen. About once every 28 days, a ripe egg cell bursts out of the **follicle** that has nourished it and leaves the ovary. The ripe egg is swept into the nearby **fallopian tube** by fluids and by tiny hairlike cilia on the inside of the tube.

Fertilization, the uniting of a mature egg cell with a sperm cell, almost always happens in the fallopian tube. Immediately the covering of the egg cell changes to block the entry of other sperm. The new cell that has been created moves slowly into the **uterus.**

In a mature woman, the uterus is about the size and shape of a large pear. The walls of the uterus are made of extremely elastic muscles, able to stretch to an enormous size during **pregnancy.** These same powerful muscles contract downwards to make childbirth possible. They also contract during **menstruation,** sometimes causing cramps in some women.

The **vagina,** or birth passageway, is a tube also made of elastic muscle. The walls of the vagina touch each other most of the time, much like a collapsed balloon. During sexual excitement the vagina expands and produces a lubricating fluid that makes **intercourse** easier.

The **cervix,** or neck of the uterus, which opens into the vagina, is made of muscles that close tightly during pregnancy, but stretch enormously during childbirth. No human engineer could design such a perfect system for beginning and supporting a new life! It's another miracle by God, the master Designer!

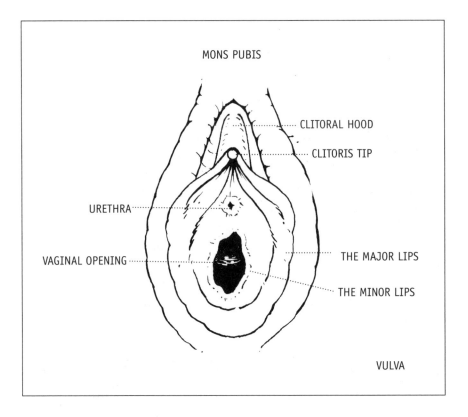

MONS PUBIS

CLITORAL HOOD

CLITORIS TIP

URETHRA

VAGINAL OPENING

THE MAJOR LIPS

THE MINOR LIPS

VULVA

The Vulva, or External Sexual Organs

The opening of the vagina is partly covered by the **hymen,** a membrane that is broken the first time sexual intercourse occurs. At one time an unbroken hymen was an important proof of **virginity.** We now know that it often is broken much earlier in life without the girl realizing it. Because some hymens are thicker than others, many women choose to have theirs checked by a doctor and stretched or cut if necessary before they are married.

Surrounding the opening to the vagina are two fatty folds of skin, the labia majora (major lips). The outer sides are covered with hair. They serve as protection for the genital area.

Inside these are two more folds of skin, the labia minora (minor lips). Sometimes they are hidden by the major lips; sometimes they stick out between them. They may be pink or brown, wrinkled or smooth.

At the top of the labia minora is a small cylinder of very sensitive tissue, the **clitoris.** A woman may be able to see the pea-sized end of it with a mirror, or it may be hidden by the folds of the labia.

Between the clitoris and the vagina is the **urethra,** where urine leaves the body. It is very small and is completely separate from the vagina.

Menstruation

Which of the following common myths have you heard?
1. Menstruation is dirty because bad blood is leaving the body.
2. Menstruation is an illness. A menstruating woman should avoid exercise, especially swimming.
3. The menstrual cramps some women complain about are imaginary.
4. Women cannot handle important jobs because their menstrual cycle produces mood changes and uneven levels of energy.
5. It's difficult for teenage girls to use tampons.

The above statements are *all false.* Don't be embarrassed if you have fallen for one or more of them. They are so widely believed that nearly everyone is affected by the attitudes they represent. Because there is a kernel of truth in each of them, you need detailed, factual information to separate the truth from the myth.

Here it is:

Facts about Myth 1: The menstrual flow is a mixture of blood and cell fragments. When a ripe cell leaves the ovary, the uterus prepares for the possible beginning of a new life. Hormones (estrogen and **progesterone)** cause a soft thick lining to form on the uterus walls. Extra blood flows to the uterus, ready to nourish a fertilized egg.

When fertilization does not happen, the egg cell, the new lining, and the extra blood are not needed. They break up and flow out through the vagina. This process happens about once a month for 25–40 years. Since God makes every person unique, the menstrual cycle is a little different for each woman.

Although menstruation is a normal, healthy process, some girls are embarrassed by it, especially in the early years. This feeling usually changes when they become more used to their adult bodies.

Perhaps the "dirty" label began because of the odor that forms when air and warmth interact with the menstrual flow. If a woman keeps herself clean and changes sanitary napkins or tampons frequently, odor will not be a problem.

Facts about Myth 2: Menstruation is a sign of a healthy, normal body. Although many women have times when they feel uncomfortable during their periods, they can and should carry on normal activities. Most women feel best if they exercise moderately rather than strenuously.

Following ordinary health rules is especially important at this time: get enough rest, drink plenty of fluids, and avoid salt.

Facts about Myth 3: Menstrual pain is real but not universal. For some women, hormonal changes just before menstruation produce a variety of symptoms called premenstrual syndrome (PMS). The most common are a dull abdominal ache, a feeling of fullness, and breast tenderness. Women who notice PMS symptoms should cut down on salt, sugar, and caffeine during the week before menstruation.

Studies show that daily exercise will give definite relief to about two-thirds of the women who suffer from menstrual pain. The removal of tension also helps. Telling yourself to relax may not be the answer. However, it is important to understand that your mind and your body do work together. If you expect to feel pain, you are more likely to react fearfully to that first little cramp, with more tension bringing more cramps. So encourage yourself; remind yourself that you are experiencing a God-created readiness to bring new life into the world.

If you are one of the 5% of menstruating women who experience severe PMS symptoms, see a doctor. Doctors can prescribe drugs that may not only give relief from pain but help correct the hormone imbalance that may be the cause of the symptoms.

Facts about Myth 4: Other symptoms of PMS may include tension, depression, or fatigue. Many women feel extra energetic or exceptionally happy midway between two menstrual periods, when a mature egg leaves the ovary. The extra hormones produced at that time can boost her energy level and make her feel good all over. Two weeks later her hormone level drops—just before she begins to menstruate. She may feel tired and somewhat depressed. However, there are other body cycles that have a similar effect—and these apply to men as well as women. We all need to learn about ourselves and to adjust to these changes and make the most of every day.

Facts about Myth 5: In most girls the hymen stretches easily enough to permit use of a correctly placed tampon. Insert the tampon, following the directions on the package. (To prevent infection, it's important to wash hands first.) The tampon cannot go too far in or fall out. Relax and take your time. Nervousness may cause the muscles around the vaginal opening to tighten. Many women prefer menstrual pads, which can easily be attached to panties. They come in many different shapes and sizes.

Pads should be changed several times a day; tampons should be changed every four to six hours and should probably not be used at night. Toxic shock syndrome, a rare but dangerous illness, can be caused by not changing tampons often enough. See a doctor right away if you develop any of the following symptoms while using a tampon: sudden fever of 102 or more, vomiting, diarrhea, dizziness, fainting, or a red skin rash.

More Questions

What if a vagina is too small for a penis? (Tani, 16)

The walls of the vagina are elastic enough to permit the birth of a baby; an erect penis is much smaller. When a woman is sexually aroused, her vagina gets bigger and produces a fluid which lubricates the inner walls.

The other boys make fun of me because I have so much fat on my chest it looks like I have breasts. What is wrong with me? (Samuel, 14)

There is probably nothing wrong with you. Breast enlargement is very common among adolescent boys. It is a temporary condition and has no connection with your masculinity.

*Why do people **masturbate?*** (Lisa, 16)

Touching the clitoris, **vulva,** or penis can produce strong feelings of pleasure. When an individual does it to produce those feelings of pleasure, it is called self-stimulation or masturbation.

There have been many stories told about the harmful effects of masturbation, but there is no evidence that masturbation causes any physical harm. Persistent masturbation, however, may well be cause for concern. A young person may worry: What do I say and do on a date? What if he (she) thinks I'm weird? What if she (he) doesn't like me? Masturbation can be one way to escape these feelings of loneliness and uncertainty. It can prevent a person from dealing with these problems and solving them with the resources of caring people.

Will masturbation cause problems later in intercourse? (Denzell, 17)

There's more to intercourse than bringing body parts together. In the sexual fantasies that usually go with masturbation, someone of the other sex is a toy made for your sexual pleasure. That's not much help in learning to see that someone as a valuable person who can give and receive love. Another problem: When people learn to reach orgasm very quickly through masturbation, they may have difficulty with premature orgasm in normal sexual intercourse.

My menstrual periods have stopped. I know I'm not pregnant because I'm a virgin. What's wrong? (Pilar, 16)

If you have just started menstruating, your body is probably still working on the timing of the menstrual cycle. Many young girls have very irregular cycles. Your periods could be 28 days apart, then 36, then 91, then 27. They will become more regular as you grow older.

Menstrual periods sometimes stop for a while because of unusual stress (a new job, the death of someone close, a breakup with a boyfriend, strenuous exercise, the loss or gain of a lot of weight). If none of these explanations fit, see a doctor.

My breasts are flat, and none of the boys give me a second look. Is there something I can do to make my breasts grow? (Sarah, 16)

I'm shorter than the other guys, and my sex organs haven't developed much. Is there something wrong with me? (Tony, 14)

Sarah and Tony are people who develop a year or two later than the average. Sexual changes are triggered by each person's individual time clock. Because of this, some 14-year-olds look like adults while others, equally normal, look like children.

Even after they have completed their growing, Sarah's breasts may be smaller than many of her friends' and Tony may be shorter than many other males. Who is to say what is the right breast size or height? All of us are different. Many of us are dissatisfied, too, with some of our physical characteristics until we realize that we are lovable and loving people just as we are. God has made us different physically just as He has given us different abilities.

Why do so many people think the sexual parts of our bodies are dirty? (Kareem, 15)

Ignorance, mostly. Or maybe they haven't stopped to think about how precisely, how wonderfully, each of us is made. No wonder God thought our bodies good enough to be temples of His Spirit! He made them that way. Adam and Eve were able to be completely naked and unashamed before the fall into sin. Since the fall we have felt differently about our bodies and have had more difficulty seeing them as the gifts of God they really are.

Chapter 3

Sex and Your Health

"I need to have intercourse soon to get experience. What if I get married and can't do it right?"

"I'm too fat to be lovable."

"A few beers make me an irresistible lover. I hear that marijuana is better yet."

"It doesn't hurt to experiment a little with sniffing, smoking, popping pills, and drinking."

"It's no one else's business if I choose to smoke; after all, it's MY body."

"Nice people don't get STDs."

You probably don't believe any of these myths. But they are so common—and so dangerous—that we all need up-to-date information about each of them.

Inexperience

Myth 1: *"I need to have intercourse soon to get experience. What if I get married and can't do it right?"*

Some young people may worry unnecessarily about not being able to "do it right" when the time comes. But most of the time that is an excuse.

People do need to learn how to have intercourse—but two inexperienced married people can learn together. They do need practice—considerate, mutually satisfying practice, which is difficult to have outside the security of marriage, and which God forbids outside of marriage.

Overweight

Myth 2: *"I'm too fat for anyone to love me."*

To be lovable, a person really needs to be loving. God daily gives you the power to be a loving person when He pours out His limitless, unconditional love for you. In Jesus, His Son, He forgives you and calls you His own child.

However, people who are heavier than average often feel so miserably self-conscious that it is very hard for them to take the risk of reaching out to other people.

Mark has been overweight for as long as he can remember. He always walks to classes by himself. He is so afraid of being rejected he won't even join someone who is also alone.

By the time Mark gets home from school, his loneliness and boredom push him straight to the kitchen. He carries a plate heaped with food to the family room, where he watches TV until supper.

Many people are like Mark. To them, food brings relief from feelings of anger, depression, nervousness, or boredom. They know, deep down inside, that they are just making their problem worse, but they can't seem to stop themselves.

Christy eats as much as Mark does on some days, but on others she doesn't eat at all. Sometimes she even forces herself to vomit to get rid of the huge plateful of food she has just eaten.

Even though Christy is so thin her bones stick out, she sees herself as fat. Her goal is to look like the super thin models in her favorite magazine. When she looks in the mirror, she sighs over her "thunder thighs" and "hippo hips"; she hates the way she looks.

Eating disorders are a fairly common problem among young women today; they starve themselves and/or overeat compulsively. The current fad for skinny models sends the message that a sexy and desirable body *must* be slim. Not true! Good-looking people come in many shapes and sizes. Good health is attractive; dull eyes and hollow cheeks are not.

One thing that happens as people mature is that they learn to put less emphasis on physical appearance in rating themselves and others. Think about the happy, well-loved adults whom you know. How many of them look like magazine models?

Christy's and Mark's basic problem is not fat but how they feel about themselves. They need to remember that since God truly loves them, they have good reason to love themselves. In the power of God's love for them, they can take responsibility for their own happiness. They can decide to think and do whatever lifts them up, instead of constantly putting themselves down.

Mark can praise himself for his accomplishments in algebra and in learning to play the trumpet. He can choose to do something after school that will make him feel good about himself: go for a long walk, eat an apple instead of a bag of chips; offer to help the new kid in math class with his homework.

Christy can remind herself that she is often very sympathetic and helpful to friends who come to her for advice; she needs to have the same compassion for herself. Maybe her goal of a "figure like a model" is a way of demanding impossible perfection from herself—something she would never do to a friend.

As Mark and Christy realize that **"before the world was made, God had already chosen us to be His in Christ"** (Ephesians 1:4 TEV), they will begin to like themselves again—and be free to choose not to let food rule their lives.

When Mark or Christy is tempted to binge on huge amounts of food, he/she can ask, "If I do that, how will I feel afterwards?" If Christy finds herself glaring at the mirror and thinking about skipping dinner, she needs to decide whether self-hatred and fasting will really make her feel better—short-term and long-term. If binging and fasting make you feel both physically uncomfortable and disappointed in yourself, why not do something else instead? Enjoy the feeling of being in control of your own life!

Reaching out to others who share your problem is often a big help if you are trying to turn your life around. Ask your doctor to recommend an eating disorder clinic. Look up Overeaters Anonymous or Weight Watchers in the phone book; ask whether a teen would feel comfortable in the group nearest you. Ask about cost too. The clinic may be covered by insurance; Overeaters Anonymous is free.

Overeaters Anonymous is especially for people who can't seem to stop overeating. The OA principles are based on the 12 steps made famous by Alcoholics Anonymous. "We admitted … that our lives had become unmanageable … We made a searching and fearless moral inventory of ourselves." (We note what we eat, how much, and what our real reasons are.)

One more point. If you ask God to help you change your eating habits, you may feel even more guilty if you fall off your diet—You might say to yourself: "My faith isn't strong enough." God knows how hard it is for you; He forgives all kinds of failures in our lives. He will give you the power to forgive yourself and like yourself no matter what size you are. His love for you has nothing to do with how much you weigh. If you decide that dieting is not for you, that decision has no effect on your relationship with Him. Fat or thin, you will always be a valuable person in His sight.

Alcohol and Drugs

Myth 3: *"A few beers make me an irresistible lover. I hear that marijuana is better yet."*

Alcohol

Establishing a happy physical and emotional relationship with another person is not easy. It's not surprising that people are anxious to believe that drugs like alcohol will help make it easier. But medical evidence shows that alcohol is not a stimulant; it is a depressant. Why does a drinker imagine he is being pepped up when he is really being slowed down?

Alcohol works first on the brain area that controls judgment and thought. The drinker is more relaxed, thinks fuzzily, has difficulty making decisions.

If a person wants to trap someone—or be trapped—into making a choice he or she would not make while thinking clearly, alcohol is a useful crutch. However, most of us would rather not begin a new relationship of any kind under those circumstances.

Drinking too much can make a man temporarily **impotent.** The problem usually disappears when he sobers up. However, if impotence is related to a longtime habit of heavy drinking, the problem may be a permanent one.

God's Word reminds Christians that we don't need to get drunk. We have a better alternative: **"Do not get drunk with wine, which will only ruin you; instead, be filled with the Spirit"** (Ephesians 5:18 TEV).

Marijuana

Many people incorrectly believe that marijuana is a sexual stimulant. What it really does is distort a person's picture of reality. Anything that a user believes is true becomes temporarily real for him or her.

Evidence from one study suggests that male marijuana smokers may be more likely to be impotent than nonusers. Another study found a definite link between heavy marijuana smoking and reduced levels of sperm and of the male hormone testosterone.

Ephesians 5:18 is a good text to remember also when you're faced with the temptation to use marijuana or any other harmful drug.

Addiction

Myth 4: *"It doesn't hurt to experiment a little with sniffing, smoking, popping pills, and drinking."*

Nobody ever intends to become addicted to a drug. People plan to experiment a little and then walk away. It works for some. We all know someone who decided one day to quit smoking and has never looked back. Unfortunately, we also know people who have tried many times to escape from an addiction; they succeed for a while and then slip back into the old habit.

Genetic research shows that some of us are more likely to become alcoholics than others. There has been much less study of the links between genetic factors and addiction to tobacco and other drugs. However, the available evidence suggests that the same **genes** might also make a person more vulnerable to other addictions. At this time there is no way to find out whether you are a person who is extra vulnerable to alcohol or other drugs.

Roughly 50% of the forces that say yes or no to addiction are provided by environment and by one's own decisions. The people who are most likely to have an alcohol or drug problem are those who feel they need to drink or use another drug to help them through difficult situations.

"I feel so self-conscious at parties. When I'm drinking, I can talk to anybody."

"I smoke pot to escape the pressures of my life, the problems I have at home and at school."

"When I drink, I don't care about my worries."

We all have pain in our lives. We all have times when we feel lonely or stupid or afraid. Learning to cope with those painful feelings takes time and effort and a continual turning to Jesus. Chemical crutches do not help in the long run.

Next time you feel down, remember that you are not alone. Others are struggling with the same feelings, even though they wear carefree masks. Jesus was an adolescent once. He had the same temptations, fears, and growing pains you face. He understands how you feel. You can talk to Him about it and ask Him to help you. As you depend on His help, you can handle anything.

Drugs and Unborn Children

Myth 5: *"It's no one else's business if I choose to smoke; after all, it's MY body."*

Your body is a gift from God. If you choose to, you can shut Him out of your life.

But the secret of enjoying your body is to give it back! St. Paul urges us to **"offer your bodies as living sacrifices, holy and pleasing to God—this is your spiritual act of worship. Do not conform any longer to the pattern of this world, but be transformed ..."** (Romans 12:1–2).

Another point to consider: The body you have been given has within it the mysterious power of conceiving new life. Decisions you make now about your body have a profound effect on children you may have in the future.

A **fetus** gets the food and oxygen it needs from its mother's body. If harmful chemicals are present in her body, the fetus receives them too. If the mother is addicted to a drug, such as cocaine or crack, the newborn baby will also be addicted.

Drugs can have a different effect on the fetus than they do on the mother. Certain widely used tranquilizers (downers) and amphetamines (uppers) can cause birth defects. Even aspirin can be dangerous, taken in the wrong quantities and/or at the wrong time.

Pediatricians say that tobacco is responsible for more health problems in babies than any other drug. It causes babies to be born too early and weigh too little. These premature infants continue to gasp for air after they are born, victims of the carbon monoxide in the mother's bloodstream. Smoke in the air around the baby doubles the child's risk of ear infections, asthma, and SIDS (sudden infant death syndrome).

Babies of mothers who drink heavily are often born with fetal alcohol syndrome, a condition that limits both mental and emotional development. Doctors advise mothers not to drink at all during pregnancy.

Sexually Transmitted Diseases

Myth 6: *"Nice people don't get STDs."*

What are STDs?

Sexually transmitted diseases, or **STDs,** are diseases that are usually passed from one person to another by close sexual contact.

The most serious STDs are **AIDS, gonorrhea, syphilis, genital herpes, chlamydia, trichomoniasis,** and **human papilloma virus** (HPV). Although a yeast infection can be passed on by sexual contact, it is not considered an STD because it has many other possible causes.

Why are STDs dangerous?
- People may have an STD without realizing it.
- Infected people are misled when symptoms disappear temporarily. However, the symptoms usually come back, worse than before.
- Some consequences of untreated STDs are blindness, arthritis, mental illness, **sterility,** cancer, and/or death.
- Babies born from an infected mother may have major birth defects.

How does a person get an STD?

The bacteria, viruses, or parasites that cause STDs live on the warm, damp surfaces of the body. The diseases are most often spread by intercourse or intimate sexual activity in which these surfaces touch each other.

Because the **HIV** (AIDS) virus also lives in blood, HIV can be spread through contaminated needles used for "shooting" drugs. In the 1980s a few people caught HIV through blood transfusions. Today's testing methods make it almost impossible to get HIV in this way. AIDS cannot be passed on by ordinary social contact.

Babies can be born with AIDS, syphilis, or genital herpes. Syphilis can be caught by kissing a person who has contagious mouth sores at that time. Gonorrhea can be caught by touching infected sexual organs if one's hand has a break in the skin. Trichomoniasis can be passed on by moist towels, bathing suits, or a damp toilet seat. In all these cases the infected person may not ever realize that he/she has an STD and can pass it on to others.

How can I tell if someone has an STD?

You can't. Only a well-informed doctor can tell. A person with a contagious case of an STD may appear perfectly healthy. On the other hand, the symptoms described in the section on STD specifics have many other possible causes. You could do someone a great injustice if you assume that his/her illness was caused by an STD.

How common are STDs?

More than one million people in the U.S. and Canada are infected with the HIV (AIDS) virus. Annually, one million new cases of gonorrhea occur. Syphilis is at a 40-year high. There are four million new cases of chlamydia every year. Ten to 30% of 15- to 19-year-olds are infected. There are now 24 million cases of HPV, with a higher prevalence among teens.

STD SPECIFICS

AIDS

What are the symptoms? (All people may not notice all symptoms.)

Most people have no early symptoms. The human immunodeficiency virus (HIV) that causes acquired immune deficiency syndrome (AIDS) attacks a person's immune system and damages his/her ability to fight disease. Without a functioning immune system, the person becomes vulnerable to many life-threatening illnesses, such as meningitis, pneumonia, and cancer. Symptoms of these "opportunistic" diseases include persistent cough and fever associated with shortness of breath or difficulty in breathing and multiple purplish blotches and bumps on the skin. Early symptoms may include fever, diarrhea, weight loss, tiredness, and swollen lymph glands.

How soon do the first symptoms appear?

A few weeks to 10 years or more.

What happens if the disease is not treated?

There is no known cure for AIDS. Most people who carry the HIV virus look and feel healthy, since it may take as long as 10 years before a person with HIV develops AIDS. AIDS is almost always fatal.

What will the doctor do?

Diagnosis: Blood test for HIV infection.

Treatment: No cure now known, although some medical treatments can delay many of the illnesses associated with AIDS. The AIDS virus is not transmitted by ordinary social contact, but through the exchange of contaminated blood, as in using "dirty" needles in "shooting" drugs, and the exchange of body fluids in sexual intercourse. Therefore avoid drug use and avoid sexual intercourse outside of marriage.

Gonorrhea

What are the symptoms? (All people may not notice all symptoms.)

Pain or itching when urinating; frequent, urgent need to urinate. White or yellow discharge from penis or vagina. Sore penis or vulva; sore throat.

Most women and some men have no early symptoms. Their only hope is that their sex partners will tell them they may have been infected.

How soon do the first symptoms appear?

Two to seven days after exposure. Early symptoms last about two to three weeks.

What happens if the disease is not treated?

Men: The germs spread through the body. If untreated, they can cause any or all of these problems: abscess in prostate gland; swollen, painful testicles; sterility; kidney damage.

Women: The infection usually centers in the cervix, spreading to all other sexual organs and may cause painful abscesses that leave scar tissue. The scar tissue often blocks fallopian tubes, making pregnancy impossible or very dangerous.

Both men and women may get acute arthritis and eye infections.

What will the doctor do?

Diagnosis: Examine sex organs. Take a sample of discharge from penis or cervix.

Treatment: Give penicillin or tetracycline by injection or by mouth. One dose is usually enough, but some strains of gonorrhea have developed that are resistant to penicillin.

Syphilis

What are the symptoms? (All people may not notice all symptoms.)

Stage 1: A sore (usually painless) on the penis, vulva, around the rectum, in the mouth, or on the lips. The sore is at the spot where the infection entered the body.

Stage 2: A rash (sometimes very faint). May turn into sores in warm, wet areas. Temporary hair loss. Swollen glands.

How soon do the first symptoms appear?

Stage 1: 10–90 days or more after exposure. If left alone, the sore will go away within six weeks.

Stage 2: Three weeks to three months after the sore goes away. Without treatment, these symptoms go away within a few weeks or months.

What happens if the disease is not treated?

The patient's syphilis will remain hidden for months or years. Only a blood test can detect it. After 2–40 years have passed, the following symptoms may occur: large destructive sores; heart problems; paralysis; insanity; irreparable damage to the baby during pregnancy.

What will the doctor do?

Diagnosis: Examine serum from the sore under a microscope. Take a blood test.

Treatment: Give an antibiotic. Regular blood tests necessary for one year.

Chlamydia

What are the symptoms? (All people may not notice all symptoms.)

Sixty to 80% of women and 50% of men with chlamydia have no early symptoms. Symptoms, when they appear, are similar to gonorrhea (see above).

How soon do the first symptoms appear?

Usually three weeks after infection.

What happens if the disease is not treated?

Men: Inflamed urethra and testicles. Possible inflammation of rectum. If untreated, sterility.

Women: Infected urethra and cervix. May cause infertility, pregnancy in the fallopian tube, or inflammation of the pelvis. It's possible to infect newborn babies.

What will the doctor do?

Diagnosis: Examine tissue or cell cultures.

Treatment: Give an antibiotic by injection or mouth.

Chlamydia germs can live in the body for years without causing noticeable symptoms. Faithful married couples are often shocked to learn that they both have chlamydia, caused by a sexual episode in one partner's past.

Genital Herpes

What are the symptoms? (All people may not notice all symptoms.)

Blisters or small bumps on penis and urethra or cervix, vagina, and vulva that may break and form open painful sores. Often the blisters are so small the person does not realize he/she has the disease and can pass it on to others. There may be pain when urinating. With the first infection there may also be fever, joint pain, flu-like signs, itching, and tingling.

How soon do the first symptoms appear?

Two to 20 days after exposure. May go away and reappear months later, even if there has been no sexual contact in between.

What happens if the disease is not treated?

May cause birth defects or death for a baby whose mother has herpes. There is strong evidence of a link between genital herpes and cancer of the cervix. Yearly Pap tests are advisable.

What will the doctor do?

Diagnosis: Check to be sure it is not syphilis.

Treatment: Salve on infected area will make the patient more comfortable. Researchers are still looking for an effective cure.

Human Papilloma Virus (HPV) (Genital Warts)

What are the symptoms? (All people may not notice all symptoms.)

Warts on the genital organs, from the size of a small tick to the size of a cauliflower.

How soon do the first symptoms appear?

Varies from a few weeks to years.

What happens if the disease is not treated?

The HPV virus may cause cancers of the cervix, vagina, vulva, and penis.

What will the doctor do?

No treatment can get rid of the virus, but the warts can be treated or removed surgically. Often they reappear.

Trichomoniasis

What are the symptoms? (All people may not notice all symptoms.)

Women: Yellowish-green smelly discharge; pain in pelvic area; soreness or severe itching in vulva.

Men: Most have no symptoms. Thin, whitish discharge, especially in the morning; tingling, itching sensation in penis.

How soon do the first symptoms appear?

Four to 28 days after exposure.

What happens if the disease is not treated?

The tiny parasites that cause "trich" will probably continue to multiply and cause discomfort. There is a link between trichomoniasis and cervical cancer.

What will the doctor do?

Diagnosis: Analysis of discharge.
Treatment: Medication taken by mouth.

Other Questions

How can a person tell if he/she has an STD?

An examination by a doctor is the only way to find out for sure. If you notice any of the symptoms, see a doctor as soon as possible. An STD is easier to stop if it is diagnosed early and correctly. Do not try to treat yourself with antibiotics or other medicines. Each disease requires a different treatment.

There are other possible causes for most of the symptoms. For instance, pain during urination may be caused by a kidney or bladder infection. A discharge from the vagina could be perfectly normal or it could be a yeast infection (not an STD). If you are in doubt, see a doctor. Knowing for sure that you do not have an STD is important for your peace of mind.

Where can I go for help?

Here are some possibilities:

- *Your parents.* Most parents are loving, supportive, and forgiving when their teenagers come to them with major problems.
- *Your local public health STD clinic.* Look under your city or county name in the phone book. A public clinic is sometimes crowded and impersonal, but you are likely to find caring and competent people there. Public health doctors see so many STD cases that they become experts in their treatment. There will probably be no charge.
- *Your family doctor.* Level with the doctor. Without information only you can give, he/she may not suggest an STD as the possible cause of your symptoms.
- *A trusted school nurse or school counselor.* They will know where you can go for diagnosis and treatment.
- *Your pastor.*

Are you immune to an STD after you have had it?

No. The same person can get it again and again.

How likely am I to get an STD?

If you use your sexuality responsibly and wisely, you have very little chance of becoming infected. It's important, however, to inform yourself about STDs because

- you may need to advise and counsel friends who are less well-informed;
- it is possible—though unlikely—for a person who is not sexually active to get an STD;
- an untreated STD could destroy not only your life, but the lives of your mate and your baby.

Chapter 4

Loved, I Love

"I wish I weren't so shy (clumsy, ugly, stupid)."

"Why should other people like me? Most of the time I don't even like myself."

"I know my sins are forgiven for Jesus' sake. But I don't always FEEL forgiven. I still feel guilty."

"If only I had a steady, everything would be different."

"I know God loves all people. But I am only one insignificant speck compared to the millions of people in the world. I need someone who will care about ME as a person, someone who thinks I am important."

Jesus Demonstrated God's Love

One of Jesus' jobs here on earth was to demonstrate to you that God loves you in a very personal way. A leper—Levi the tax collector—a widow—Simon the Pharisee—a prostitute—Jesus made each of them feel important: each of them felt loved.

How many teachers would bother having class if there was a big snowstorm and only one student was there? And yet if you page through the Gospel of Luke you'll notice that Jesus spent a lot of His time teaching or healing just one person.

When you share feelings or problems with God, remember that you are very special in His sight. Incredible though it seems, you have His undivided attention. You don't have to do anything or be anything to get Him to love you. He just does—and He always will. He **"did not spare His own Son, but gave Him up for us all— how will He not also, along with Him, graciously give us all things?"** (Romans 8:32).

Loved, I Love: Practical Strategies

Key Words

"Through Christ, God makes me His own son/daughter."

A Situation

Maria stands alone near a group of girls who are waiting for class to begin.

OLD Destructive Response

"I wish I could be their friend. I wish someone would see me and ask me to join them."

NEW Creative Response

"If God values me so much, why shouldn't they? I don't have to try to take over their conversation to make them notice me. I'll just be their friend."

Key Words

"There is more to me than my defects."

A Situation

Randy hates summer. Because he is so tall and skinny he thinks he looks ridiculous in shorts. Of course he gets year-round teasing about his big feet.

OLD Destructive Response

"No point in going swimming when I look like such a freak."

NEW Creative Response

"There is more to me than big feet and bony knees. I have a good sense of humor, and I'm a loyal friend. I can't change my feet, but maybe I'll try weight lifting to build up my muscles. And today I'm going swimming."

Key Words

"God gives me talents."

A Situation

Jenny has an appointment with the manager of a local gift shop. At least 20 girls have applied there for a summer job. Only one will be hired.

OLD Destructive Response

"She's probably already picked somebody. With all this competition I don't have a chance."

NEW Creative Response

"If I were the manager, I'd want a person who is honest, pleasant, hardworking, and dependable. My success in getting baby-sitting jobs proves I meet the last three requirements. And I must have a reputation for honesty, 'cause I'm often asked to take care of the car-wash money for the church youth group. God gave me these talents. I know I'd do well in that job!"

Key Words

"I know who I am."

A Situation

Brad would like to go around with the "in" group at school. But he is uneasy about some of the things that happen at their parties.

OLD Destructive Response

"If I don't go along, they'll laugh at me. Everyone else does it, so it can't be that bad."

NEW Creative Response

"I know who I am—a person in whom Christ lives. Sure, I want to be part of the group, but not at the price of letting them make decisions for me."

Conversation with Steve:
Anger, Guilt, and Jealousy

I guess I just can't make it as a Christian. I've got this terrible temper that just won't stop. There's no way I can control it!

For instance?

Last night I half-killed my brother Pete, just because he borrowed my new shirt without asking. That's the worst fight we've ever had, but it isn't the first.

Do they usually start like that? Pete does some little thing you don't like, and then you get mad?

I guess so. But it really isn't my fault. Pete acts so superior sometimes, just because he's the lucky one in the family. Everyone thinks he's wonderful because he's smart and good at sports and has the girls falling all over him. He not only thinks he's God's gift to women, but he has the nerve to flirt with MY girl friend! And he's always borrowing my clothes without bothering to ask. I TRY not to get mad. But I can just hold it in so long, and then I explode! If Pete were more considerate, it wouldn't happen. So it's HIS fault.

Guilt is a very uncomfortable feeling, Steve. People often try to escape feeling guilty by pushing their share of the blame onto someone else. Could that be happening to you?

I guess so. I really feel rotten when I think how much I hurt Pete. And my parents are disappointed in me, too.

Have you talked with God about it?

No. How can I go back and ask for forgiveness again? I keep doing the same thing over and over. If I want to be forgiven, I should stop losing my temper. It's hopeless.

Remember the story of the Prodigal Son (Luke 15:11–32)? The runaway boy was just as ashamed of himself as you are. The sensible thing for his dad to do would have been to take him back on probation: "You can come home if you shape up." But the father ran to meet him, put a ring on his finger, gave a party! That's the way your Father in heaven feels about you.

Even if it's the 27th time I've come home?

That's right. God's love for you does not depend on good behavior, for **"While we were still sinners, Christ died for us"** (Romans 5:8).

I can't believe that God approves of my behavior.

You are right. He loves you always—that's why He may not approve of all your behavior. He wants you to grow more loving in what you do. He also cares about your parents and your brother, and doesn't want you to hurt them.

But how can I change? I've tried and tried, but it doesn't do any good!

Daily invite His Spirit to live in you and work through you. If you fail sometimes, keep coming back for more forgiveness. Remember, even St. Paul complained that **"What I do is not the good I want to do; no, the evil I do not want to do—this I keep on doing"** (Romans 7:19). So there is a power inside us, leading us to sin. But we have God's own power too. **"That power is like the working of His mighty strength, which He exerted in Christ when He raised Him from the dead"** (Ephesians 1:19–20). Stop trying so hard and yield yourself to the fantastic power God gives you as His forgiven child.

You mean it will be easy to control my temper if I have enough faith?

I didn't say that. But your faith is your basic equipment. Trusting God, you can use the thinking ability He gave you. When you stumble, you can learn from your experience. He'll help you, too, to study the strategies other Christians use to handle feelings like anger, and then experiment to find what works for you.

Practical Strategies:
Dealing with Anger, Jealousy, and Guilt

A Situation

Pete borrows Steve's clothes without asking.

Possible Responses

Destructive Choice: Hides anger, even from himself. Often leads to a big blowup later.

"I won't say anything. It's not worth arguing about. I'm really not very angry anyway."

Creative Choice: Tells Pete how he feels before he loses his temper.

"Pete, I intended to wear that shirt myself last night. Next time I want you to ask me first. If I'm not here, please find something of your own to wear."

A Situation

Pete flirts with Steve's girlfriend, Kristen.

Possible Responses

Strategy 1: Steve tells Pete and/or Kristen how he feels. Might work—but Steve has other options if he doesn't want to do that.

Strategy 2: Steve talks it out with a friend—or goes for a long walk and talks to himself. "What am I really afraid of? That I'll lose Kristen to Pete? Do I really think that would happen because of 15 minutes of kidding around? No, not if Kristen and I have as good a relationship as I think we do."

Strategy 3: Steve uses hard physical exercise to release his anger. He throws a basketball against the side of a building, goes for a long hard run, or pulls all the weeds in the garden. Or he pounds his mattress, whaps a towel against the bathtub, goes off by himself and yells or cries—anything to get rid of the anger before it becomes destructive.

Strategy 4: Steve prays. God has heard angry feelings before. (Some of King David's psalms sizzle with his anger: **"May their eyes be darkened so they cannot see, and their backs be bent forever. Pour out Your wrath on them; let Your fierce anger overtake them"** (Psalm 69:23–25). Once Steve has unloaded his feelings, he can ask God to give him power to act with love and understanding.

Key Words

"I can admit to myself and to God that I—like most people—feel jealous sometimes."

A Situation

Steve realizes much of his anger is caused by his jealousy of his brother. He feels that most people (including their parents) like Pete best.

Possible Responses

Strategy 1: Because jealousy is often caused by self-hate, Steve reminds himself that God gives each person different gifts. He asks God to help him learn to appreciate his own special qualities.

Strategy 2: Jealous people often are so busy putting themselves down they don't accept love or compliments from others. "Next time somebody says something nice about me," Steve tells himself, "I won't act like they're either stupid or insincere. I'll just smile and say 'thank you.'"

Strategy 3: Steve risks talking to his parents about his feelings—not accusing them of favoritism but just telling them how he feels. ("I may be wrong but …")

Sometimes two children in the same family are treated differently for reasons that have nothing to do with the youngsters themselves. For instance, if Steve's dad is worried about his job right now, he'll show less patience with Steve's low grades this semester than he did with Pete's school problems last year. Usually the inequalities balance out, but we all tend to remember the time when the other person came out on top—and forget the time when the advantage was in our favor.

Key Words
"I can fail without being a failure."

A Situation

Pete says something nasty about Steve's girlfriend, Kristen. Steve gets angry and starts swinging. Pete's head hits the corner of a table. Cost: 37 stitches and a ruined, blood-soaked leather jacket.

Possible Responses

Destructive Choice 1: "He had it coming. I don't feel one bit sorry!" (People often make this choice because they think choice 2 is the only other possibility.)

Destructive Choice 2: "That settles it! I'm no good and never will be."

Better Choice: "Pete should not have said what he did. But that's his problem."

Christian Response: "I am responsible for my own actions. So I'll do my best to make things right with Pete—buy him a new jacket and do his chores until he's feeling better. It's good to know that God never gives up on me, but always forgives and lets me have another chance."

Conversation with Tracy: Love and Freedom

I'm glad God loves me. But I need somebody human to love me too.

God knows that. His love is the source for human love. Because He loves you, you can risk reaching out to others. You can love and be loved.

But that's what I want! I wish I had a boyfriend.

Is a boyfriend the only possible source for love in your life? What about your family and your other friends?

All my girlfriends have boyfriends.

And you feel left out. That's natural enough. But if you date just so that *you* will feel accepted and important, you are *using* your date.

What do you mean?

Well, when you like a person for himself or herself, good things can happen. But when you see a person as a means to an end, a way to get what you want, you not only destroy the relationship but whatever you get isn't worth much.

Sometimes I'm afraid to face that, I think. I figure I'd better hang onto a boyfriend—even if he's just using me—because if he breaks up with me I'll really feel alone and worthless.

Most of us do have times when we feel like that. The thing we have to get through our heads is that Christ took all that aloneness, all that worthlessness on Himself. All we have to do is turn away from looking inward and center our lives on Him. Then, He promises, **"You will know the truth, and the truth will set you free"** (John 8:32).

Free?

Free in Christ. Free to look at yourself honestly and objectively. Free to accept yourself as you are. Free to love and be loved. Free to change. Free to *grow* as God's son or daughter.

Chapter 5

Dating

Does a person have to date to be considered normal?

How does one get started dating?

Is dating only one person a good idea?

What is the best way to handle a breakup?

How much physical contact is okay?

What if we've already had intercourse?

Questions, questions. There are sure a lot of them when it comes to dating.

Help from the Bible

Do you think the Bible has all the answers?

Why don't you do some reading—check it out for yourself? You will not find a Bible text that answers specific questions like, "How does one get started dating?" But you'll sure find guidelines that will help you make decisions.

I don't like being preached at, though.

Who does? But that doesn't make God's law any less true. "The wages of sin"—also sexual sin—"is death." God's Word is very clear about that. The Bible is pretty specific in labeling sexual sins—and warning Christians about them. For example, **"God will judge the adulterer and all the sexually immoral"** (Hebrews 13:4). Or: **"Flee from sexual immorality. All other sins a man commits are outside his body, but he who sins sexually sins against his own body"** (1 Corinthians 6:18).

The great thing, though, is that God doesn't just give us warnings. He stands at our side to *help* us. Notice, for example, how that Corinthians passage goes on: **"Do you not know that your body** is a temple of the Holy Spirit, who is in you, whom you have received from God? You are not your own; you were bought at a price. Therefore honor God with your body" (1 Corinthians 6:19–20).

What does that mean, "You were bought at a price"?

St. Peter put it this way: **"For you know that it was not with perishable things such as silver or gold that you were redeemed … but with the precious blood of Christ"** (1 Peter 1:18–19). *Jesus loved us enough to die for us!* That's what our Christian faith is all about.

It does help me to remember that Jesus loved me that much! And that He gives me His Holy Spirit.

It puts a new light, too, on the false value that says, "Try not to hurt anyone—but if it feels good, do it!"

Yes, that kind of life-style ignores who I am—as a Christian, I mean.

It sure does. You are more than a body. St. Paul lays it on the line when he says: **"Live a life of love, just as Christ loved us and gave Himself up for us … among you there must not be even a hint of sexual immorality, or of any kind of impurity … because these are improper for God's holy people"** (Ephesians 5:2–8).

That's a lot to live up to.

It's a way—the only way—to be really free. We don't have to do "what everyone else is doing." We're able to say either yes or no— remembering who we are as God's own people—and counting on His forgiveness when we fail.

Great! But could we get to some of those specific questions about dating now?

Getting a Date

I've been saying "Hi" all semester to a guy in my English class, but that's as far as it goes. How can I get to know him better?

Greeting someone with a big smile is a good start. Some days, try to leave class at the same time he does. Ask him a question about the homework assignment; tell him the rumor you heard about the next test; joke with him. You might gradually become better friends, until one of you suggests doing something together— maybe as a part of a larger group.

It could be, though, that as you get to know each other you'll find you really don't have much in common. That's why it's smarter not to pin all your hopes on one person. Your best bet is to make friends with many people.

It took me weeks to work up courage enough to ask Tracy for a date. She turned me down. What's wrong with me?

Why does there have to be anything wrong with you? If she acted sorry that she couldn't make it, ask her to something else. If she turns you down again without suggesting a different time, etc., forget her.

Everybody is rejected at one time or another. (That's why it's so great to know that God keeps on loving us in Christ!) If you think of something you said or did that may have cooled her interest in you, learn from that. Don't worry about it—her "no" was most likely caused by her interest in someone else or by some other problem in her life.

Value yourself. Remember that you're God's own person. You will find other girls who do appreciate you.

What can I do to make myself more popular?

Many psychologists have conducted experiments that try to find out the reasons why some people have more friends than others. Besides the basic principles we talked about last chapter, the researchers turned up some other factors.

They discovered that the most popular people are those who like others and are pleased when others like them. Yet they are not terribly worried if someone doesn't. (Interesting, isn't it, how this relates to what God intends for us: that we grow as *loving persons!*) The more relaxed you are, the better you will do in a social situation. Don't allow yourself to worry and fret about what people will think of you. *Expect* them to like you. Why shouldn't they? Concentrate instead on getting to know *them.*

The researchers also found that people make friends with those they see often in pleasant circumstances. You're not going to meet many people while you are in your room at home.

It's nice to be popular. There are times, though, when the price is too high. Sometimes it's necessary to choose between doing the right thing and being liked by the group you are in at the time. Often the choice is easier than it looks. The first person to speak up and say "I don't think this is a good idea" may be surprised by the number of others who have been thinking the same thing.

After six weeks of looking at Kathy all during history class, I finally asked her out. It was a disaster—neither of us had a good time. What went wrong?

You probably didn't have very much in common. Next time choose a girl you feel comfortable with, a girl who seems to enjoy your company. If you don't know any girls that well, look for a group of guys and girls who do things together. Some people are active members of two church youth groups because the groups have so many activities.

Is there anything wrong with going out on a blind date?

It depends on who arranged the date. A friend whose judgment you trust will have a pretty good chance of picking someone you'd enjoy spending an evening with. But when you don't know anyone in the group very well, you are risking an unhappy, embarrassing evening.

What about a pickup date?

There's a real chance of getting hurt—perhaps badly hurt. No one is wise enough to be an instant judge of character. Pickups are often people who want instant satisfaction. Unwilling to spend time and effort building a relationship, they seek "fun" on a one-night-stand basis.

Dating More Than One Person

Paul (whom I like fairly well) asked me to the prom. I don't want to accept and then have Ryan (whom I like very much) ask me. What should I do?

How would you feel if you were Paul? Would you want to be kept dangling as a "spare" date in case the first choice isn't available? If you want to take your chance on Ryan, give Paul a fast, kind "no, thank you." You don't have to tell him why unless you want to.

If you decide to say yes, play fair. Stick to your yes no matter what happens. If Ryan asks you, you can suggest doing something with him another time.

Is it all right to tell a boy that you like him a lot? I 've only gone out with Jim twice, but he already means more to me than any other boy ever has. My friends tell me to play hard to get, but that seems so dishonest.

Playing games with people's feelings *is* dishonest. It's silly to pretend to be standoffish unless you really feel that way.

However, you can choose between several ways of letting Jim know you like him a lot. You can push for a steady relationship he's not ready for. If you do, he may be embarrassed and irritated—and might drop you.

A choice made by many girls is to express their feelings by encouraging sexual intimacy. That's even more dishonest; it's pretending to have the deeply committed permanent relationship people have in marriage. Pretending won't make it true. Most of all, such sexual intimacy is wrong because it leaves God out of the relationship. (Remember all those specific Bible texts we looked at in the beginning of this chapter.)

The best way to let Jim know how you feel about him is to appreciate him. Tell him the strengths and talents you have seen in him. Notice the thoughtful things he does for you; be kind and considerate of his feelings.

Is there something wrong with me because I don't want to date?

Many young people do little or no dating during their teen years. These nondaters usually have friends of both sexes, and they spend time with their friends.

The group gets together for parties, basketball games—whatever. Sometimes closer friendships form within the group—people find others they can talk to, confide in.

The most interesting groups are very flexible about their membership. New people are welcome, and no one is pressured to participate in any one activity. Often one person will belong to several informal groups. It's a no-hassle way to become more comfortable with people of the other sex.

A girl I've taken out a couple times asked me to a pool party. I wear a brace on one leg. After I remove the brace, I can swim fairly well, but my leg is thin and funny-looking. Will my handicap make a difference to her?

It depends on the girl. Some girls would admire you for dealing with your handicap. Others might be embarrassed and uncomfortable (their problem, not yours). The safest plan might be to tell her about your leg now, so she has time to get used to the idea. Be matter-of-fact, not apologetic. If you have a positive attitude about yourself, chances are others will also.

My father won't let me go to a girl's house when her parents aren't home. When a girl comes to our house, we're not left alone for more than a few minutes. Why doesn't he trust me?

Maybe he trusts your integrity and your dependability but is a little uneasy about your judgment. Being alone with a person you like can be very exciting. It's tempting to let things go further than you intended.

That doesn't mean that your body will take over and you will be unable to stop yourself. It is always possible to stop—but it may be very difficult. Your father may also be concerned about your reputation and that of your date.

Why should I have to watch out for my reputation just because I'm female? My mother keeps nagging about clothes and makeup that might give people the wrong idea about me. But the guy next door does whatever he wants and nobody criticizes him. It isn't fair!

I can appreciate how you feel, but the Bible doesn't make any distinction between men and women when it calls Christians to be as lights in a dark world. How else will people come to know about Jesus—except from Jesus' people? And how interested will they be in what we have to say if we have a bad reputation?

I didn't intend to go out only with Sandy, but everyone assumes we are a couple. We've gone out three weekends in a row. I don't want to hurt her, but I don't like this trapped feeling. How do I get out?

Take the risk of sharing your feelings with Sandy. Be sure to make it clear that you really do enjoy her company.

Maybe Sandy has been feeling trapped too. You might be able to work out an arrangement that permits you to see each other without either person feeling tied down.

It's good to get to know a lot of different young women. Why? You'll find out which qualities are important to you in a woman. When the time comes that you are ready to marry, you will choose more wisely.

Dating Only One Person

My parents are furious because I exchanged rings with my boyfriend. In my high school you either go out with only one person or you don't date at all, but my parents can't seem to understand this. How can I get them to see my side?

Most people see one person for a few months, then another and another. If you see your relationship as one which is probably temporary, your parents won't worry quite as much.

Explain to your parents that dating only one person makes it easier to get together casually. As you do ordinary things together, you get to know each other very well. Managing this relationship can be good practice for marriage some day.

Of course, they're probably afraid you may "practice for marriage" in other ways. They have no way of knowing what you're thinking if you don't talk to them—and listen to them. Let them see how responsible you are about keeping any agreement you make about things like hours, unsupervised time alone together, alcohol, and the places you go.

Right now my girlfriend and I (both 17 years old) think we want to spend the rest of our lives together. But we realize we'll both change a lot in the next few years. How can we keep from getting too serious too soon?

Each of you should have some activities in which you are independent of the other—different jobs, schools, clubs—anything that will help you learn to know yourselves as separate persons. Talk honestly and openly about what is happening in your relationship. Make individual plans for the future, but remind yourselves that joint plans must be tentative. Consciously turn your bodies over to Christ. Together, ask Him to help you guard against hurting each other with too much physical intimacy too soon.

I can't help being very jealous of my boyfriend. One day a note fell out of his pocket. I grabbed it and read it. It was from another girl! It was just about their history assignment, but I was furious! Shouldn't he stop exchanging notes with other girls when he's MY boyfriend?

Do the words "MY boyfriend" mean a close, caring relationship or does it mean owning another person? Very few people are willing to have no life at all outside a relationship. Even in a marriage, most people do not read their mate's mail unless invited to do so.

Grab hold of God's love for you in Jesus. He will help you feel less insecure. (See Chapter 4 or talk to an older person you trust.)

I have been offered a summer job as drama coach at a camp about 150 miles from home. My boyfriend has a good job right here in town. If I go away, we might not see each other all summer. I need the money and the experience, but is it worth taking a chance on losing my boyfriend!

By the time fall comes, both of you will be more independent, more interesting persons. You'll have many new experiences and ideas to share. You could end up closer than ever.

Even if you stay at home, you are taking a chance that you will lose your boyfriend. People change, especially when they are young. It hurts when a friendship dies, but clinging to each other will make no difference.

If you truly have a strong relationship, it will not wither away because of a summer's separation.

I've been going with Jerome for about four months, but lately he's been talking about maybe getting married someday. Even though I like Jerome a lot, I'm not ready to even THINK about being serious. I don't want to lose him and I don't want to hurt him. What can I do?

Be honest with Jerome. Ask Jesus to help you speak your mind and heart. The conversation could be painful, but it's not fair to let Jerome believe you see the future as he does.

But what will happen if you let things go on as they are? Steady dating at a young age often leads to a teenage marriage, especially when the couple feels committed to each other. Five or 10 years later, one or both partners may bitterly regret closing off their options at such a young age and want out. Of course many young marriages do succeed (often after a rough struggle). But statistics show that teenage marriages are three times as likely to fail as are marriages of people in their 20s. By shrinking from painful honesty now, you could store up a lot more pain for both of you—and for possible children—later.

Breaking Up

I have been upset ever since Andy broke up with me. I can't eat, can't sleep, can't study. All I do is sit around and think about him. Help!

The grief that you are feeling is a powerful emotion. You probably feel that you will never be truly happy again. Talk to Jesus about your feelings. Tell Him how it hurts. You may not feel any lightening of your mood, any real sense that He is there … *but He is listening, and He does care, and it will make a difference.*

Remember that Jesus often works through other people—including you. Find a trustworthy friend you can talk to about your feelings. If possible establish a new, casually friendly relationship with Andy. When you find yourself thinking about him, remind yourself firmly that this painful time will pass— and do something else. This is a good time to get reacquainted with your family, develop new interests, make new friends.

When you do begin dating again, be cautious for a while. Your pride has been hurt. Don't rush into a new relationship; you may unconsciously be using the new person to prove you are still lovable.

Intimacy

How far can I go and still have my boyfriend respect me?

Before anyone will respect you, you must respect yourself. Instead of, "How far can I go?" try asking, "What is honest between us?"; "What is best for us?"; *"What honors us as people who belong to God ?"*

How can I tell how much intimacy I can have with a girl?

Many boys would agree with you that it is up to the girl to decide. Then the boy can follow the macho creed of "get all I can," while he depends on the girl to protect him from a relationship he's not emotionally ready for.

That's not only wrong, it's old-fashioned and immature. What do you want, a girlfriend or a mother? You don't need the girl to tell you what is right. You have God's Word for your guide.

"You were bought at a price. Therefore honor God with your body (1 Corinthians 6:20).

If you remember that the next time you are in the back seat of a car, you'll have the strength to stay in control and do what God wants you to do.

My girlfriend leads me on and then gets mad when my hands wander. Is she trying to make a fool of me?

Many girls don't realize how quickly and easily boys become sexually aroused. Tell your girlfriend that she's making it very difficult for you to respect the limits you both know are right.

I love my boyfriend very much, and I know he loves me, but I'm afraid of going out of control. What can we do?

Your mutual love can make all the difference—and your mutual love for Jesus, who loves you both. When you truly care for someone, you are not likely to put your own temporary pleasure ahead of the long-term happiness of both persons. When you believe in Jesus, His will and His love for you enters into the relationship.

Remember that the further you go along the road that leads to intercourse, the more difficult it is to put on the brakes and turn around. However, it is always possible to stop. You—and your faith in Jesus—are bigger than your feelings.

My boyfriend says he loves me more than I love him, because he's ready for intercourse and I'm not. I'm afraid I will lose him if I don't do what he wants.

You might try talking with him about your relationship to Jesus—and how important His love and His will is in your life—also your next life. If your boyfriend is a Christian, you may be able to explore together what God's Word says about fornication—intercourse outside of marriage. And about the beauty of sexual intercourse within the marriage relationship. (See Chapter 7.)

If your boyfriend is not a Christian and remains insistent, ask yourself: What kind of love for you, really, does he have—if it requires you to give up your relationship to Christ in order to satisfy his physical desires? Is it lust masquerading as love? If he's threatening to dump you unless you do what he wants—is this the kind of love you can build a future on?

Michelle and I went steady for about two years. We thought we loved each other and sincerely intended to get married someday. After we broke up I felt pretty guilty—even though we never had intercourse, we came close to it many times.

I've asked God to forgive me, and I know He has. But somehow I don't FEEL forgiven. Why do my guilty feelings keep coming back? Will I always feel guilty about Michelle, even after I marry someone else?

It is unlikely that the guilt you feel now will be a problem years later in your marriage if you realize you have faced your sin and have been forgiven; you are free to go on with the business of living.

However, you will probably always regret what happened

between you and Michelle. The love you two felt for each other was an honest, real emotion, a gift of God. But the way you expressed that emotion was both wrong and unwise.

It is foolish to assume that teenage love will last forever. Most people have so many new experiences during their teens that they almost certainly will change—in an unpredictable direction. The teenage relationship may last—but it may not.

Because you acted on the assumption that your feelings would not change, you hurt Michelle and yourself. God's forgiveness does not instantly erase all consequences. Only time—and God—can heal the emotional damage that happens when people invest so much of themselves in a relationship that does not work out.

How can I get the willpower to say "this far and no farther," and stick to it? I feel so guilty sometimes, even though I have never had intercourse.

You need to talk to God about those guilt feelings. Remember, there is no sin so terrible that you cannot ask for—and receive—His forgiveness. He will never, for any reason, stop loving you.

Whatever you've been doing that you feel guilty about—don't do it! Of course that isn't as easy as it sounds, especially when willpower is something you feel you lack. You probably have the will but not the power.

The good news is, the power doesn't have to come from you. The power comes from the Christ who died for you and rose again. He lives in you. The closer you are to Him, the more power you will have. So read your Bible, pray, commune with Him in His Supper. As you get ready to go out on a date, ask Him to be with you—and trust in *His* power, not your own.

The power He gives you is not a matter of gritting your teeth and being too serious. When things get intense on a date, often a little humor will relieve the tension. Or you can explain to your date, quite seriously, that you care too much about him (her) to let anything happen you'd both regret.

Chapter 6
Finding Out if Love Is Real

What is the difference between infatuation and real love?

Marriage is a long way off for me—if I decide to marry at all. Why think about it now?

How can we tell if our love will last?

What about these old sayings? Are they true?

"Opposites attract."

"Love at first sight—that's true love."

"A teenage romance is only puppy love."

"If you can't eat and you can't sleep, it must be love."

Will It Last?

Fifteen-year-old Josie is deeply in love with Darrel, and Darrel feels the same way about Josie. They live for the times when they are together. They have a world of their own. They feel intense excitement and pleasure each time they touch or even see each other. Is their love only infatuation—"puppy love"? No. It is real and genuine. When they promise to love each other always, they both really mean it.

Will their love last? It might. And then again, it might not. At this point in their lives, there's no way to tell. Between the ages of 15 and 21, most people change interests, attitudes, and some values. They discover new talents within themselves. They observe the way others live their lives, and make some decisions about the shape their own lives will take.

Chances are Josie and Darrel will fall in love quite a few more times before they make a final choice of a mate. Each time they will learn more about how to love, how to have a satisfying relationship with another person. They will reevaluate what is important to them. These are times to consciously ask what the will of God is for them and what part He plays in their relationship. Keeping God central will improve their feelings about each other and their understanding of what it means to be male and female.

If love is based mainly on physical attraction, it may not last long. Without mutual liking and respect to keep it alive, sexual attraction withers away.

If you are wondering whether your love is a temporary one, notice the ways in which the relationship has changed you. If people say you have changed, and not for the better—look out! But if you are kinder, more responsible, more self-confident than you were before, you've got a good thing going, at least for this stage in your life. Remember that **"in all things God works for the good of those who love Him"** (Romans 8:28). God often uses a good relationship with another person to bring out the best in those He loves.

Shopping for Someone to Love

If you were going to buy a car, you would give that purchase a lot of thought. You would find out the good and bad points of various models. You would decide which features are really important to you. Comfort? Good gas mileage? A low price? Air-conditioning? Your favorite color? Easy parking in a small space? Built-in stereo? You can't have them all, so you do a lot of thinking about your choices. You don't want to spend several years paying for a car you don't like.

Shopping sounds like a coldblooded term to apply to a human relationship. However, it's not a bad description of a good way to prepare for marriage—even if you decide not to get married at all.

Many single people lead full and happy lives. You might choose not to marry because other things (perhaps your work) are more important to you. But whether you end up getting married or not, you need to think through what you really want your life to be like.

The purpose of this "shopping" is to learn to know yourself and others as developing adults. "Comparison shopping" will greatly increase your chances for a happy marriage. As you get to know different people, you will discover which character traits are really important to you; the kinds of persons with whom you feel most comfortable and happy. You also pinpoint the qualities you absolutely could not stand in a life partner!

Shopping List for Lovers

Here is a list of qualities some people think are important in a mate. Which ones are absolutely essential? Which would you consider desirable extras? Which are you indifferent about?

able to handle disappointments
  without bitterness

able to see the funny side
  of things

adventurous

affectionate

ambitious

assertive

athletic

attractive

believes in God

can manage money

cares about other people

considerate

dependable

enthusiastic

even-tempered

forgiving

friendly

generous

gentle

good listener

good self-concept

good talker

hard worker

independent thinker

intelligent

lives his/her faith

loves parties

neat

not a quitter

open-minded

patient

popular

quiet

rich

sense of humor

sensitive, understanding

sexually desirable

shares my main interest

well-dressed

Now look at the list in a different way. The key qualities you have identified are also likely to be important to the person you might want to marry. What will you have to offer? Do you live your faith? Are you someone who is dependable, someone whose word can be trusted? Are you able to laugh at yourself, able to see the funny side of life? Do you make an effort to be considerate, to treat people as you would like to be treated? Do you try to see things from the other person's point of view?

Don't be discouraged if you do not measure up to the expectations you yourself have for a marriage partner. Work at improving your weak spots. Building on the strengths you already have, you can become a person who has many positive qualities to bring to a marriage. You can become the person God intends you to be.

Giving yourself enough time and letting yourself become a little more mature will be helpful. It's well to remember, though, that age is no guarantee that people will make wise choices in love. Songs and literature often tell of mature people who made foolish choices. How then can a couple tell whether or not their love will last a lifetime? Here are some love signs you can watch for, some ways to test the durability of your love.

What Do We Have in Common?

The bad thing about our shopping list is that the same words mean different things to different people. Most of us would say we want an intelligent mate. But what we probably mean is that we'd like someone who is about as intelligent as we are, someone who has had about the same amount of education. When two people of unequal intelligence try to discuss anything, both are likely to feel bored and frustrated.

The same thing is true of many other words on the list. To one person *adventurous* might mean a willingness to try a new restaurant (provided a friend recommends the place). To another person, *adventurous* might mean a spur-of-the-moment decision to move to Montana with no job, no money, and three children. There's nothing wrong with either of those attitudes, but those two people surely will have things to work through if they marry.

Often couples are attracted to each other by their differences. If you are a quiet, shy person you might enjoy going out with a "life of the party" type to help overcome your shyness. Don't count on it working though. What often happens is that the quiet one is dragged to parties by the social one, or the social one sits unhappily at home with the quiet one.

Another common difference is family background. What will happen if Lori and Vaughn fall in love? Vaughn's family life is lively, warm, and loud. Vaughn is the only one who has graduated from high school. There isn't much money, but there's always an extra bed for a cousin from the country or a foster child who needs love.

In Lori's family, books and travel have always been important. Both of her parents have interesting, demanding careers. They are active in church and community affairs. Home is a quiet, restful place for relaxed conversation and listening to music.

Many couples as different as Vaughn and Lori have built happy marriages—and many more have failed. Couples who are thinking of marriage should spend as much time as possible with each other's families. Differences may grow smaller as they get to know each other better. Or they may find the differences eventually kill the love they shared. What one enjoys as a novelty doesn't always satisfy as a steady diet.

Will Marriage Change Us?

One of the things Julio loves about Maria is her enthusiasm. Whatever Maria does, she goes all out. Right now she's all wrapped up in dancing. Determined to be a professional dancer, she spends all her free time practicing—plus some time her parents want her to spend on homework and family responsibilities.

"She'll settle down after we are married," Julio figures. "Of course she'll want to continue dancing, but she'll also want to work. Maria's love for me is stronger than her love for dancing."

Julio may be in for a surprise. It's unfair of him to attach unspoken conditions to his love for Maria. Although people can change, it's unrealistic to suppose that getting married will make it happen. Julio and Maria need to talk frankly about what each of them expects from marriage.

It's good that Maria has been open with Julio about the family conflicts caused by her intense desire to dance. Love often makes a person conceal some qualities or interests, lest they cause rejection by the loved one. That is both unwise and dishonest. It's important to set standards of appreciation, consideration, and unselfishness you are willing to live with for the rest of your life.

God's Holy Spirit enables Christians to grow in all the qualities that make a marriage a growing and happy relationship: **"love, joy, peace, patience, kindness, goodness, faithfulness, gentleness, and self-control"** (Galatians 5:22–23).

Communication

In the best marriages communication begins long before the couple heads for the church. Many hours need to be spent on the building of a friendship, talking about

your faith in Christ;
your complete life histories;
your feelings about yourselves, your families;
your interests, your sexuality, your goals.

There's more to communication than sharing life histories and future plans. Communication starts with activities, loving listening to everyday problems and feelings. Here's an example of what we mean:

Nancy was late getting to the football field. Everything had gone wrong during the day. The final straw was when she was stuck at a railroad crossing with a freight train stopped in the middle of it. She was angry and upset with herself. She raced to the stadium gate, where Greg paced up and down looking at his watch.

Greg: Hi, honey! How's it going?

Nancy: OK, I guess.

Greg: Where've you been? The game's about to start. Hurry, let's get to our seats.

Nancy: Don't rush me!

Greg: It's bad enough being late. You don't have to be nasty about it!

Nancy: Find someone else to sit with. I'm going home!

Nancy probably hadn't even admitted her angry feelings to herself. Greg had no idea what was going on inside her head—until it was too late!

What if Nancy had kept in touch with her own feelings? And if Greg had listened in a loving way? What might have happened then?

Greg: Hi, honey! How's it going?

Nancy: Terrible. I feel mad at the world.

Greg: You had a bad day?

Nancy: You know that math test I was worried about? I flunked it.

Greg: You began the day with bad news, huh?

Nancy: And then, in English class, Mrs. Hobson jumped all over me because the girls next to me were talking. I didn't have time to argue with her after class because I had to go straight to work. And then we were so busy I had to work an extra 30 minutes. I knew I'd be late for the game! And then I was stopped by a train.

Greg: No wonder you were upset.

Nancy: I sure was. But I feel better talking about it. Thanks for listening.

What Happens When We Fight?

People who are in love still do have disagreements just like anybody else. Some couples are afraid to talk honestly. "If I tell her about that, she'll be angry." "If I tell him what I've decided to do, he'll try to stop me." Each tells the other only what he or she wants to hear. Each is very careful to cover up problems before they cause any unpleasantness.

When a disagreement does surface, each person may be surprised and hurt by the other's "unreasonable" anger. And terrible, wounding things are said by both persons.

Talking through disagreements is a lot easier than letting them get to the point where something that may be relatively minor tears you apart. But as Christians you can trust each other to not intentionally hurt each other. And you can offer forgiveness to each other when you slip and say or do something to hurt or offend.

The secret is learning to make conflicts work for you instead of against you. You will become a little closer each time you settle a problem in a way both partners can live with.

There are several ways to deal with conflict. For example, one person may give in:

Marshall: Let's go to the movies tonight.

Latrice: I really had my heart set on staying home, but if it's important to you to go out tonight, I'll go.

Or it may be possible to work out a compromise that meets both people's needs:

Marshall: Let's go to the movies tonight.

Latrice: I really had my heart set on staying home, but if it's important to you to go out tonight, I'll go.

Marshall: I'd like to go out, but if you want to stay home, maybe I
    will come over and watch a movie on television with you.
Latrice: That sounds like a pretty good idea.

Sometimes you will not be able to agree on certain issues. That
can be a real test of your love and trust for each other. It's a time to
say, "I love you even if I don't agree with you." If you can practice
this kind of acceptance with people around you, it will be a lot easier to do in a marriage relationship. You don't always have to agree
about everything. (Of course, if the issue involves a matter of right
and wrong, a clear command of God, you will want to keep on wit-
nessing for the right, striving lovingly to change the other person's
point of view and praying for God's Spirit to work through your
witness.)

Can We Talk to Each Other with Complete Honesty?

One of the joys of a good relationship is having someone to talk
to. The freer you feel to share about yourself with another person
the closer you will feel toward that person. All of us are at different
levels, though, when it comes to what we think is complete honesty.
You may want to share your innermost thoughts. The other person
may have to think through an issue before sharing it with anybody.

What if We Belong to Different Churches?

The question may be, Can a marriage work if the partners are of
a different religion? Yes, but it's not easy. The ideal is to be equally
committed to Christ and both belong to the same church so that you
can share your faith completely. Christ should be the cornerstone of
a relationship—certainly of a marriage. It is unfortunate when one
or the other cannot share Him because of differences in belief or
denomination.

*Remember that if you want a Christian marriage, marry a committed
Christian.* A marriage that is built on a deep trust in and communion
with God is like no other relationship on this earth. When both
partners seek God's will in their lives, they are not alone in their
struggle to make their marriage work. Their shared faith is the basis
for all goals, all values, all decisions. God provides them with the
strength they need when trouble comes; He guides them to the
abundant life He wants for all of us.

Chapter 7

When Two Become One

What actually happens in sexual intercourse?
What difference does marriage make in a sexual relationship?
How often does a married couple have intercourse?
What is the secret of a happy marriage?

What Happens in Sexual Intercourse?

Sexual intercourse is more than placing the penis in the vagina. There is a time before intercourse when the couple stroke, touch, gently massage, and kiss each other's bodies. This is called **foreplay.** Ideally, they have talked about what arouses each of them and know which areas of the body to stimulate. These areas, called **erogenous zones,** are a little different for each person. Typically they include the sex organs and the areas around them, the nipples, inner thighs, mouth, lips, neck, earlobes, eyelids—all areas with many nerve endings. As the couple becomes more and more excited, heartbeat and blood pressure go up dramatically. Muscles tense. In some people, a measles-like flush covers part of their bodies. In about 60% of men and nearly 100% of women, nipples become erect and enlarged.

Blood rushes into the man's penis and stays there, making it erect and hard. The woman's vagina expands and produces a lubricating fluid that makes intercourse easier. The muscles at the entrance to the vagina relax. Her clitoris enlarges at first, flattens out, and then seems to disappear under the fold of skin that ordinarily covers most of it.

When both partners are ready, they work together to guide the penis into the vagina. As the penis moves back and forth inside the vagina there is friction on the clitoris caused by the movement of the labia.

Their excitement may build until one or both of them experience orgasm. The man's penis ejaculates semen; the woman's vagina contracts and expands several times; they tremble with intense physical and emotional pleasure.

Then all of the signs of arousal go away. A feeling of well-being and complete relaxation floods their bodies. This can be a special time of tenderness when they can lie in each other's arms, caressing and talking.

Is It Always like That?

No. Different couples have different preferences about such things as foreplay and position during intercourse. There are many variations.

People have described intercourse as thrilling—soul-stirring—boring—shocking—deeply satisfying—painful—wonderfully comfortable—humiliating—confidence-building—disappointing—fascinating—disgusting—delightful.

How can the same experience be so different for different people?

God intends intercourse to be a superbly joyous way to express mature committed love between a man and a woman. In many different places the Bible speaks very positively of sexual intercourse—always within marriage. (Different words are used to describe sex outside of marriage.) Does this mean that sex within marriage always feels wonderful, and sex without marriage always feels terrible?

It isn't quite that simple. Researchers are finding that sex without commitment tends to be flat and joyless compared to sex within a good marriage. Notice the word "good." Marriage alone does not do it. More is necessary.

What Things Make a Difference in Sexual Pleasure?

The couple's total relationship controls their ability to give and receive sexual pleasure. Before intercourse can be the great experience it is meant to be, couples need to have complete trust, complete confidence in each other. They need to know that they are loved. Then each is free to suggest having intercourse, and each can say "some other time," without the other feeling rejected.

If a man and a woman try to use intercourse to become closer to each other, they will be disappointed. It works just the opposite. In intercourse, a couple celebrates the unity, the concern for each other's needs, that already is there.

Even within a good relationship, the quality and intensity of a sexual experience varies greatly from one time to another. Sometimes the pair will come to orgasm together, sometimes separately. Sometimes one person will enjoy intercourse, but will not come to orgasm at all.

For most people, the most important part of a sexual relationship is emotional intimacy. Their deepest needs are met by tenderness, closeness, and sharing.

Couples sometimes use a "how to" book about sex as a report card rather than a guide. If their experience does not follow the book, they feel like failures. These feelings matter. Fear of failure can interfere with the normal physical reactions of the body. Fear can prevent a man from having an erection; it can keep a woman's vagina muscles so tight that intercourse is nearly impossible. Guilt caused by previous sexual experiences can have the same effect.

Love ... "Till Death Do Us Part"

"Love is patient,　　Eager though we may be to have needs met and dreams fulfilled, we do not demand instant satisfaction to all our desires. We remind ourselves that a relationship that does not continue to grow is dying. Ours will grow—because our marriage is worth our energy and attention.

love is kind.　　We will always listen to each other. We will call on God's power to work within us as we try to understand and meet the other's needs.

It does not envy,　　Daily, we'll tell and show each other "you are the most important person in my life." Secure in the other's love, we will not allow lesser relationships to threaten us.

it does not boast, it is not proud.　　Because we recognize that all talents and successes are gifts from God, neither of us needs to "win," to be the most important one in the world's eyes.

It is not rude,　　We will give each other the same politeness, consideration, and attention we give to a most honored guest.

it is not self-seeking,

For each of us, the other's needs will be as important as our own.

it is not easily angered,

Recognizing that irritability is often caused by suppressed anger or worry, we will try to be open with each other about how we really feel. Because we care about each other, we will control words and actions that might hurt the other.

it keeps no record of wrongs.

Sometimes we will fail; sometimes we will hurt each other. But as forgiven sinners we can forgive those wrongs without getting even and without keeping score.

Love does not delight in evil but rejoices with the truth.

Because Christ lives in us, we can encourage each other to study His Word and live in His light.

It always protects, always trusts, always hopes, always perseveres.

We give total, lifelong commitment to this marriage and to each other. Even if bad times come, we will not give up; we will struggle and pray and love and grow.

Love never fails."

We are one in Christ—forever.

1 Corinthians 13:4–8

Why Does a Piece of Paper—A Marriage Certificate—Make a Difference?

The marriage certificate is a public commitment to make the relationship work, "for better or for worse." You say to each other, "No matter what happens—I will be there. If a child is conceived, we accept responsibility for that child—together."

Some people are afraid of marriage since it means total commitment and total vulnerability. If you choose unwisely, you will be badly hurt. But if both partners hold back a little, afraid to risk too much of themselves, complete intimacy will not happen—emotionally or sexually.

God intends that a man and a woman will **"become one flesh"** (Genesis 2:24) in marriage. This God-given oneness in sexual intercourse does not necessarily happen overnight. Sometimes years of loving communication and continual adjustment are needed to reach a completely satisfying sexual relationship.

Outside the security of a lifetime commitment, any problem triggers anxiety—and the anxiety itself can be a barrier to sexual performance.

How Often Does a Young Married Couple Have Intercourse?

There are such wide differences between individuals that it is impossible to come up with a definition of what is normal.

Even for the same person, sexual desire will vary. Much depends on how one feels on a given day. As years go by, urgent physical needs often give way to the desire for a more complete but less frequent, emotional and physical experience. On the other hand, a woman's **sex drive** may be stronger when she is in her 30s and 40s. Most men and women are physically capable of sexual activity until death.

Building a Good Marriage

So many marriages are unhappy. How can we make ours a good one?

Build your marriage on Christ; then it will not crumble when trouble comes. Jesus promised that **"where two or three come together in My name, there am I with them"** (Matthew 18:20). Of course, this is true in any group of Christians, but think of the power His promise adds to the intimate relationship of marriage! God works in and through each partner, helping each to find the true meaning of love, **"that your joy may be complete"** (John 15:11).

St. Paul compares Christian marriage to Christ's relationship with us, His church (Ephesians 5:21–33). Christ's love is the model for the love we are to have toward our mate: love that gives itself away, love that does not depend on the other doing anything or being anything, love that is totally without strings, love that does not have to be earned in any way.

Of course Christians, like anyone else, are affected by the times in which they live. Old-fashioned marriages were far less likely to end in divorce than marriages today. Each person had clearly spelled-out duties, and neither expected more than a reasonable amount of comfort and security.

People today expect marriage to be a loving, deeply intimate joining of two equal partners. That's much more demanding than the old-style marriage. The partners must work together to set realistic goals for themselves:

When will we have children? How many? How will we care for them?

How will we handle our money? How will we decide what we can afford? What if we disagree?

How will we divide household tasks? Will we do it the way our parents did or develop our own patterns?

Where will we live? Will we both have careers outside our home? How will we share in leisure activities? What material things (house, cars, etc.) do we want? How will we make sure we make God a part of our home? What will we do to serve and praise Him?

Once you have chosen your goals, you will need to decide which ones are most important. Some goals probably must be sacrificed or postponed to make others possible. When you decide to have children, you will have to look also at what the commitment to being a parent means for each of you.

Once decisions are made, the solutions are not necessarily permanent. Children have different needs at different stages. People change. Situations change.

Submit to one another out of reverence for Christ.

Ephesians 5:21

Chapter 8

When Two Become Three

When should we have a child?

How often do babies have birth defects?

Will my baby look like me?

What happens in childbirth?

What different kinds of birth control are there?

Questions about Becoming Parents

When is the best time to start a family?

For one child, you must be ready for a 24-hour-a-day, 18-year commitment. If you want several children, more years are involved. They can be very good years if you are physically, emotionally, and financially ready for each child. Do not plan on your parents or anyone else taking part of the responsibility for your child—such arrangements often fall apart after a short time. There is a difference between paying for child care (even if you pay a relative, you are still responsible) and depending on someone else for help (making them responsible.)

Children are delightful, loving, cuddly charmers. They also whine, have nightmares, fight with each other, and test your patience to the limit. Since children are immature, it is important that parents themselves be mature. God both blesses us and teaches us through our children. As we respond to our children's needs, we find we can be wiser, more patient, more unselfish than we would have thought possible.

The best time to have children is when you are secure in your relationship as husband and wife and have thoroughly worked through the financial, emotional, and spiritual commitment necessary to be both a good marriage partner and a good parent.

Having a child to give a gift to your partner or to strengthen a shaky marriage is the wrong reason and can cause many problems for you, your partner, and your child.

How can a woman tell whether she's pregnant?

Doctors look for an increase in the size of the uterus and the breasts. The cervix may be softer and may have a bluish tint. They also test the blood or the urine for a hormonal change that can be detected about 10 days after conception.

The woman may have noticed any or all of these symptoms: a missed period, breast fullness and tenderness, prebreakfast nausea, unusual tiredness, frequency of urination. However, all these symptoms may have other causes. It is possible (but unusual) for a pregnant woman to have a normal period.

While home pregnancy tests are readily available today, their accuracy rate is only about 80%. Since early diagnosis of pregnancy is very important, it is far better to see a physician. There are many substances—medicines, cigarette smoke, alcohol, drugs—that can severely damage the developing fetus. Pregnant mothers who are in top physical condition have much healthier babies and are less likely to have problems themselves.

Why are some couples unable to have a child?

In many cases the causes of infertility are unknown. Some people delay childbearing until their 30s or 40s, decreasing somewhat their chances of conceiving a child. There are a number of diseases and infections that can damage the reproductive organs. However, couples who fail to conceive within the first two years of unprotected intercourse have a better chance than ever before of achieving conception. If they seek treatment, many will succeed in conceiving.

What happens after the egg and the sperm meet in the fallopian tube?

The fertilized egg fastens itself to the cushiony wall of the uterus. A thin, tough bag forms around the egg. It is filled with a watery liquid called **amniotic fluid**. The developing baby (called an **embryo** at this stage) floats in the liquid, which protects it from bumps or changes in temperature.

At the end of two months, the embryo has a brain, eyes, ears, heart, liver, arms, legs—not fully developed yet but recognizable. After the eighth week, the embryo is called a fetus. By this time, a flat network of blood vessels, the **placenta,** has formed on the uterus wall. Mother and fetus have separate bloodstreams. The placenta is close to the mother's blood vessels so that food and oxygen can filter through it to the **umbilical cord** and on to the fetus. Waste materials take the same route back to the mother's bloodstream.

During the third and fourth months, nails begin to form on fingers and toes. Sex organs develop. The mother has the thrilling experience of feeling a little flutter inside her as the baby moves. As the fetus continues to grow, the mother's uterus and abdomen stretch to many times their original size. She becomes more and more conscious of the baby moving inside her.

What causes birth defects?

Some defects are inherited; others are caused by outside factors such as drugs, infection, STDs, alcohol, smoking, poor nutrition, radiation, or pollutants. The risks are greater for pregnant women under 18 or over 35. Early diagnosis of pregnancy is important because commonly prescribed medicines may be harmful to a developing fetus. The father's exposure to some chemicals on the job can cause birth defects in babies conceived while the chemical remains in the father's body.

Women who have what is called Rh-negative blood cells also risk birth defects in their second pregnancy. If the fetus has Rh-positive blood, the mother's body will attack the fetus' red blood cells. This can be prevented by vaccination after the birth of a first baby (or after a miscarriage).

Everyone should have a complete physical examination before marriage. For women, the exam should include blood tests to check immunity to rubella and to find out blood type. Babies born to mothers who have rubella (German measles) during pregnancy often have serious birth defects. Doctors recommend that girls be vaccinated against rubella long before they conceive a child. A woman should not become pregnant until at least three months after vaccination.

What is a premature baby?

Some babies are born before the nine months are up. If a baby is born more than a month early, she (he) will probably weigh less than five and one-half pounds. Babies that small may need special care to survive. A baby weighing less than two pounds has only a small chance of survival, although new medical techniques now make it possible for doctors to save smaller and smaller babies.

What is a miscarriage?

Sometimes a fetus does not develop properly, so the uterus pushes it out of the body. This is called a miscarriage and is most likely to happen during the second or third month of pregnancy. We don't know the causes for all miscarriages, but some are due to virus infections or drugs.

How is the baby's sex decided?

All human cells, including sperm and egg cells, have 23 pairs of **chromosomes.** The chromosomes each contain many genes, different characteristics that are passed on to the next generation. About half of a man's sperm cells have a male chromosome; the other half have a female chromosome. The question of male or female depends on which sperm happens to reach the egg cell first.

What decides color of hair, musical ability, intelligence—all the things people inherit from their parents?

People inherit possibilities from their parents—hair that will be shiny black if clean and healthy, intelligence and musical ability that may or may not be developed. Most of us inherit far more natural talent than we ever use. However, all these possibilities are in the new cell that forms when the sperm meets the egg. A woman's body makes hundreds of egg cells in her lifetime, each with a different combination of genes. Some genes carry characteristics she does not have herself, such as red hair like her great-grandfather's.

A man's body makes millions of sperm cells in his lifetime, each with a different combination of genes from his family. The baby's characteristics will depend on which sperm cell meets which egg cell. One of the special wonders of parenthood is seeing some of your own characteristics blended with those of the person you love best, creating a totally unique individual.

What happens in childbirth?

Powerful muscles in the uterus contract for 30 seconds or so, then relax. The contractions feel like a mild menstrual cramp and are about 15–20 minutes apart at first, but gradually become stronger and closer together. The uterus is slowly pushing the baby downward. At some point, the bag of amniotic fluid breaks and the liquid flows out through the vagina.

Gradually the cervix opening expands from about one-eighth inch to about four inches. More contractions push the baby down into the vagina. The mother contracts her abdominal muscles to "push"; often the father helps by holding her and/or encouraging her. Many parents-to-be attend classes that prepare them for this moment.

The baby's head usually appears first, then one shoulder followed by the other. The doctor guides and supports, but never pulls, the baby.

When the baby is breathing normally, the umbilical cord is cut about three inches from the abdomen. In time the stump will dry up and fall off, leaving a navel behind.

Its work finished, the placenta is now expelled from the mother's body. The entire birth process ordinarily takes about 8-20 hours for a first child.

Is childbirth painful?

Pregnant women who are well-informed about what to expect tend to be more relaxed and therefore experience less pain. Many women learn exercises and breathing techniques that give them some control over the process, and they like that. But each individual is different. No one should feel she is a failure because she needed pain-killing drugs during childbirth.

Is it harder to give birth to twins or triplets?

Not really. Because she is carrying more weight, the mother may be a little more uncomfortable during the last month or so. But the babies are born one at a time. Since they are likely to be smaller than other babies, they may need special care for awhile.

What is the difference between identical twins and fraternal twins?

Fraternal twins are conceived when two different sperm cells join two different egg cells. Although they often feel especially close to each other, they each inherited a different set of characteristics from their parents.

Identical twins are conceived when one sperm cell joins one egg cell. The fertilized cell splits into two or more cells that are exactly alike, and each of these divided cells grows into a separate individual.

Although identical twins begin life with the same set of inherited characteristics, they have different experiences and make different choices. Each becomes a unique individual, exactly like no one else in the world. Each has her (his) own special relationship with God.

If children are a gift from God, why are so many new parents tired and depressed?

All new parents get tired, since the new member of the family is quite apt to sleep all day and howl all night. Caring for a new baby is a *lot* of work, especially during the first month or two. Normal hormonal changes in a new mother's body can also cause depression. Some mothers who quit jobs for parenting find it hard to get used to being at home. Some find it helpful to take a college course, do volunteer work—anything that adds some mental stimulation and adult companionship to their lives.

New parents can become upset because they don't measure up to their own ideals of what a good parent should be and do. They can't always soothe the baby when she (he) is crying. Perhaps the mother is unable to nurse the baby as she had hoped. When they stop trying to be superparents, they'll enjoy parenting more.

Sometimes new parents need professional guidance as they struggle to adjust. If you know a parent who feels anger and rejection most of the time, urge her (him) to see a pastor or contact a family service agency or the local Mental Health Association. Parents who desert or abuse their children are usually people who cannot cope and do not ask for help.

Even normal parents sometimes have mixed feelings about their baby. They love and yet sometimes they don't like him (her) very much. They may resent the changes the baby has brought to their lives or feel trapped, weighed down by responsibility. If they give each other love, understanding, and support, this shared experience will end up being a very positive one. Talking about feelings helps. So does prayer. As time goes on, the new parents will find that, although feelings of irritation and anger come and go, their love for their child is a basic, growing part of their love for each other and for God.

Birth Control

Unfortunately, the terms **birth control** and **contraception** are often used as if they mean one and the same thing.

Strictly speaking, birth control refers to anything that controls/prevents a birth. Thus it includes **abortion**—destroying a fertilized egg or embryo or fetus. Because abortion ends a human life, it is clearly contrary to God's Word—and thus is unacceptable as a birth control method.

But the common understanding of the term birth control refers to methods for *preventing* the union of sperm cell and egg cell. These methods of *contraception* (which prevent conception) do not end a human life. (The intrauterine device [IUD] and morning-after pills are *not* true contraceptives since they do not prevent the male sperm from joining or fertilizing the female ovum. Rather, they prevent a fertilized ovum from being implanted in the uterus and continuing its development and are actually abortive in character.)

Birth Control Methods (Contraception)

What is the best method of birth control?

The only perfect method of birth control is **abstinence** since women who have intercourse even once can become pregnant. A doctor can help a married couple decide on a method that will work well for them and is compatible with their religious beliefs. Since effectiveness depends on proper use, the method must be acceptable to both partners. It's best if both share the responsibility of remembering the doctor's instructions and following them exactly.

Birth Control Pills

What are they?

A series of pills that make it unlikely that a woman's ovaries will release an egg cell. To be effective, the pills must be prescribed by a doctor and must be taken on schedule. A yearly physical exam is important.

Advantages?

Convenient to use. Very effective.

Disadvantages?

Many women have unpleasant side effects that may include nausea, weight gain, irregular or painful menstrual flow, sore breasts, rash, headaches, intolerance of contact lenses, depression, or nervousness. For a few users there are serious side effects including high blood pressure, heart attacks, strokes, blood clots, and gall bladder disease. The greatest risks are run by women who smoke heavily, have any undiagnosed uterine or vaginal bleeding, or a history of heart or liver disease. There is also an increased risk for women who smoke and women who are over 35.

Reliability?

Out of 100 women, fewer than one will become pregnant in one year if the pills are used as directed.

Spermicidal Chemicals

What are they?

Spermicidal chemicals destroy sperm and block sperm from entering the cervix. They are available without a prescription at drugstores. The most effective form is aerosol foam, which is placed high into the vagina with a plastic applicator. Spermicidal creams and gels are effective when used with a condom or diaphragm.

Advantages?

No serious side effects. Protects against some (not all) STDs.

Disadvantages?

Allergies to chemicals cause tissue irritation in some people.

Reliability?

Out of 100 women, six will become pregnant in a year if the method is used correctly.

Male Condom

What is it?

A thin latex (rubber) or lambgut sheath that covers the penis during intercourse and catches the semen. Can be bought in a drugstore without a doctor's prescription.

Advantages?

Effective, especially when used with a spermicide. The latex condom (not the lambgut) offers some protection against some STDs, but provides no **safe sex** guarantee.

Disadvantages?

Care is needed to prevent the condom from tearing or coming off. Some men say that condoms reduce the pleasure of intercourse.

Reliability?

Without spermicide: Out of 100 women, three will become pregnant in one year if condom is used according to package instructions. With spermicide: Out of 100 women, fewer than one will become pregnant in one year if condom and spermicide are used correctly.

Barrier Methods: Diaphragm, Cervical Cap, Female Condom, Contraceptive Sponge

What are they?

Both the disk-shaped diaphragm and the cup-shaped cervical cap are made of thin rubber and fit over the cervix. Both must be used with a spermicide.

The female condom is a polyurethane sheath with a flexible ring at each end. One ring is at the closed end of the sheath and fits over the cervix; the other remains outside the vagina and covers the vulva.

The contraceptive sponge is a small, pillow-shaped sponge that has been treated with a spermicide. The sponge is moistened with tap water and then inserted high into the vagina. It has a ribbonlike loop for easy removal.

The condom is intended for one-time use, while the other barrier devices provide continuous protection for 6 hours (diaphragm), 24 hours (sponge), or 48 hours (cap).

Advantages?

No serious side effects. Reduces risk of STDs; the female condom provides the most protection. The female condom and the contraceptive sponge are disposable.

Disadvantages

Some women might not bother to use the device every time. A doctor must prescribe the correct size of diaphragm or cervical cap and must give thorough instructions for use. These devices must be inspected regularly for breaks or tears; they should be replaced periodically. If the contraceptive sponge is incorrectly inserted, it may be difficult to remove.

Some women experience more frequent urinary tract infections. Allergic reactions can cause vaginal irritation. A sponge, cap, or diaphragm that is left in too long can, in rare cases, cause toxic shock syndrome. Research has not yet proven how long is "too long," but women using this method should be aware of TSS symptoms: sudden high fever, vomiting, diarrhea, dizziness, or a red skin rash.

Some couples say that the condom dulls the pleasure of intercourse.

Reliability?

Out of 100 women using a diaphragm, six will become pregnant in one year when the diaphragm is used properly.

Out of 100 women using a female condom, five will become pregnant in one year when the condom is used properly.

Out of 100 women using a cervical cap or a contraceptive sponge, nine will become pregnant in one year when the user follows directions exactly. When either of these two methods is used by a woman who has already borne a child, the likelihood of pregnancy doubles.

Natural Family Planning

What is it?

Conception happens only if intercourse takes place just before or just after an egg cell is released by an ovary—about seven days a month. If the woman can figure out when her "unsafe" period is, she does not have intercourse during that time. She takes her temperature every morning (it rises when the egg is released) and/or checks changes in her normal vaginal discharges. For success the woman must be willing and able to carefully observe, record, and interpret fertility symptoms. Couples must be willing to abstain from intercourse 10–14 days each month.

Advantages?

Some people prefer a natural method for religious or other reasons. No side effects. Helpful in planning a desired pregnancy.

Disadvantages?

Fertility awareness methods are confusing and difficult for many people. It is easy to become careless and discouraged. Both husband and wife need to have a serious commitment to making it work.

Reliability?

Out of 100 women who follow directions exactly, two will become pregnant in one year.

Sterilization

What is it?

In women, the fallopian tubes are cut so the egg and sperm cells cannot meet. In men, the vas deferens is cut so that sperm cannot mix with the semen. For both women and men, sterilization does not interfere with any sexual process other than the ability to conceive new life. Women continue to menstruate; men continue to ejaculate.

Advantages?

Freedom from further birth control measures and from the fear of pregnancy often adds to sexual pleasure.

Disadvantages?

If a person changes his (her) mind, reversing the operation is difficult.

Reliability?

Out of 100 women or men (only one partner need be sterilized), there will be fewer than one pregnancy in one year.

Note: Most statistics taken from *Contraceptive Technology*, 1994.

Chapter 9

Tough Questions

What actually happens in an abortion?

How can a sexy magazine or an R-rated movie possibly hurt me?

How can I protect myself against rape?

Why do promiscuous people act the way they do?

What causes homosexuality?

Most of this chapter zeros in on questions you have probably thought about at one time or another. The questions cover a wide range of topics.

Can sperm swim through jeans?

Not if they're on. Social workers who operate a telephone question-answering service report that this is the most common question asked by teen callers. It is very unusual for a woman to get pregnant without sexual intercourse. However, it is a possible result of heavy stimulation. If sperm are deposited on the vulva, they may travel into the vagina and on through to the uterus to a fallopian tube.

Many unwanted pregnancies have begun when people had sexual intercourse in what they've been told is a "safe" way or when they use birth control methods incorrectly.

Pregnancy *can* happen
—the first time a person has intercourse.
—after intercourse in any position.
—on *any* day of a woman's menstrual cycle.
—even though the woman does not come to orgasm.

A woman *cannot* prevent pregnancy by
—taking a birth control pill that morning.
—jumping up and down after intercourse.

—putting a tampon in the vagina first.

—**douching** (washing out the vagina) with cola or anything else (can cause an infection).

A man *cannot* prevent pregnancy by

—using plastic wrap or a plastic bag to catch the semen.

—withdrawing his penis just before ejaculating. (This method sometimes works but is very unreliable because sperm can leave the penis before ejaculation.)

I'm not married, and I think I am pregnant. What should I do? Where can I go for help? I CAN'T tell my parents.

Right now you are probably feeling panicky—guilty—worried sick. Maybe you think you have destroyed your relationship with your parents—or even your relationship with God. Are you wondering whether your parents will ever forgive you? Will God forgive you?

God will. Talk to Him about what you have done and how you feel. Jesus didn't even scold the woman caught in the act of adultery. Instead, He protected her from those who would harm her and sent her home with the words **"Leave your life of sin"** (John 8:1–13).

Jesus will forgive both you and the baby's father—and gladly welcome you back. Remember the Lost Sheep (Luke 15:1–7). Jesus will stick by you in the difficult months ahead.

Remember too that God works through other people—your parents, for instance.

If you feel unable to talk to your parents right now, some other possibilities are

• a pastor or church youth worker,
• a school counselor or school nurse,
• your family doctor or a doctor at a clinic.

Professional ethics—and, often, state laws—forbid any of the professionals listed above from telling your parents without your consent. However, whoever you talk to will probably urge you to confide in your parents without delay, for the following reasons:

Your parents are likely to be more supportive, more helpful, more forgiving, than you think. Yes, they will be angry and hurt at first. But they will be even more hurt when they find out later that you have shut them out of this crisis in your life.

They are almost certain to find out sooner or later. Even now, they are probably uneasily aware that something is wrong. When you lie to someone you love, you move further and further away from them. The secret makes a wall between you and people who love you very deeply.

You have some decisions to make that will profoundly affect the lives of several people, including the baby's father and your unborn child. You need help in exploring the consequences of each option open to you.

Even more important, you need to think through the moral issues involved so that someday you will look back and say, "I made the right choice." Even though your parents may be too emotionally upset to guide you, they can help you find the kind of Christian counseling you need.

A caring, professionally trained and Christian counselor can also help you, your parents, and your boyfriend understand each other better. Even when parents try hard to forgive and understand, they can't easily get rid of their feelings of anger, disappointment, and failure. This will be a very painful time for all of you, and you need all the support you can get.

My friend Mollie knows for sure she is pregnant. She says she wants to keep her baby. Is that a good idea?

That depends. Single parent families can work if the parent is well prepared for the responsibility of a child. Enough money, enough maturity, enough emotional and physical strength—all these are essential.

Some unwed mothers look forward very much to having a baby to love. "The baby will always love me," they figure. "I'd much rather take care of a baby than go to school!"

But the baby is much more work than school ever was. The longed-for love grows slowly and depends on the care and attention she is able to give the baby. There's never enough money. Jobs are scarce without a good education, but going back to school is tough to arrange when baby-sitting arrangements must be made.

Mollie could find herself trapped, permanently stuck with a monotonous and unfree life-style. And her child would suffer most of all.

Newspaper columnists like Ann Landers often print pathetic letters from young people who must deal with the problem of a much-too-early pregnancy.

Mollie and her boyfriend might decide to get married. Then the baby will have two parents.

Not necessarily. The odds are that the marriage will end in divorce.

Even if the marriage lasts, the chances of a happy relationship are slim—and both are likely to unconsciously blame the baby. Parents who feel their lives have been stunted by the responsibility of a child find it very difficult to meet that child's needs.

Should Mollie give her baby up for adoption?

Only Mollie can decide that. She must compare the love and care she is able to give her child with what adopted parents can give. Mollie's own feelings, and those of the child's father, must also be considered.

These days, many unwed mothers decide to keep their babies. If there are several unwed mothers in a school, they are likely to encourage each other to make the same choice they did. If Mollie decides to give up her baby, she may be making an unpopular decision, but one that will bring joy to a couple who may have been waiting for years for a baby. Church-affiliated adoption agencies have long been placing babies into Christian homes. However, it is certainly true that none of the options available to Mollie is without pain.

What about abortion? I hear there's nothing to it these days.

What you've heard is only partly true. Medically speaking, abortion is a simple procedure if done within the first three months of pregnancy. In many states, free or low-cost clinics make it possible for teens to get abortions without the consent or knowledge of their parents.

In other words, Mollie is free to make an irreversible decision without the support of people who love her very much. Although abortion may seem the easiest way out of Mollie's dilemma, it is not. Killing an embryo or fetus is not like having an infected tooth pulled. Mollie is dealing with a living being, created by God just as she herself was created by God. Even those who don't care about the judgment of God's Word may experience guilt and grief and psychological and emotional scars that take a long time to heal.

What actually happens in an abortion?

In early pregnancy, the most common method is vacuum aspiration. A plastic tube is inserted into the uterus. The embryo and menstrual fluids are vacuumed out. In the D & C method a sharp spoon-shaped instrument scrapes away pieces of the embryo until it is all gone. RU-486 is a drug that expels the embryo from the uterus. *Saline abortion* is often used after the first three months of pregnancy. A needle inserted into the uterus draws out some amniotic fluid. This fluid is replaced with a saline (salt) solution that kills the fetus. Within 24 hours the dead fetus is expelled from the mother's body.

What does the Bible say about abortion?

The Bible says that each of us has a special relationship with God that began *before we were born.* Jeremiah writes:

The word of the Lord came to me, saying, "Before I formed you in the womb I knew you, before you were born I set you apart; I appointed you as prophet to the nations" (Jeremiah 1:4–5).

David, the psalm writer and king, is even more specific:

You created every part of me; You put me together in my mother's womb ... When my bones were being formed ... when I was growing there in secret, You knew that I was there—You saw me before I was born. The days allotted to me had all been recorded in Your book, before any of them began (Psalm 139:13–16 TEV).

The Bible also emphasizes the value of each human life. **"Thou shalt not kill"** is one of the Ten Commandments that God wrote with His own hand and gave in a special way to His people (Exodus 20).

There is therefore no way to justify killing a human embryo or fetus—even though some claim an abortion is justified if it saves the mother (and father) from embarrassment, broken plans for the future, or emotional pain. Life is so special that God sent His own Son to be born of a young human mother so that all people could share His love on earth and have eternal life in heaven.

What is pornography?

Some of the most beautiful statues or pictures portray the naked human body. They give us an appreciation for how wonderfully God has made us. Unfortunately, humans take this beauty and distort it;

all too often we make ourselves less than we are intended to be.

If, when you look at a picture (or whatever), you can easily remember that the picture shows a special person who is valued by God—this is not pornography. **Pornography** happens when a human is displayed as a sex object, a thing to be used for someone else's pleasure. Pornography makes us feel dirty, uneasily guilty about our sexuality, instead of proud and grateful that God has made us male or female.

Is it really wrong to just look? How can a picture, magazine, or movie hurt me?

Where did your Christian attitudes, opinions, and values come from? You weren't born with them. Indeed, God's Word reminds us that we all have an inborn leaning toward sin. (See, for example, Ephesians 2:3 and 4:22.) On the basis of the Bible we call this "our old sinful flesh." We know, too, from God's Word that the devil seeks to work through the "world"—the evil influences all about us—to lead God's people to sin and lack of trust in God.

By Baptism God made us His own children—forgiven people who by the power of the "new man" are called to resist the devil and the sinful world.

The question then is: Is pornography part of the "world," which appeals to our sinful flesh? Or is it part of God's good creation, which appeals to our new nature and builds our spiritual life?

Pornography, in other words, can pollute our minds in the same way sewage pollutes a river.

What's wrong with R-rated movies? What if the movie is just frank and open, not dirty?

The best way to tell whether a movie is harmful is to notice the effect on your thinking. Does the movie picture a world in which God exists? Does it substitute a slick "get all you can" philosophy for honest love? Does it tear down or build Christian values?

Sometimes explicit language has a slightly different meaning from the more polite words. Constant use of street words for sex can make intercourse seem a hostile act instead of a way to express committed love.

We can decide whether to eat roast beef or garbage. We also have the power by God's Spirit to choose what goes into our heads and hearts.

Right. It's MY head, MY body. If I happen to get a kick out of a mildly dirty magazine, that's MY business.

God has not given you absolute ownership of your body.

Do you not know that your body is a temple of the Holy Spirit, who is in you whom you have received from God? You are not your own; you were bought at a price. Therefore honor God with your body (1 Corinthians 6:19–20).

What is a flasher? Is he dangerous?

Flasher is a slang word for an **exhibitionist,** a person who gets sexual satisfaction from showing his (her) genitals to others. The typical flasher is a man who delights in shocking young girls. Exhibitionists should be reported to the police so they can receive psychiatric help.

What if a woman is raped?

Rape happens when one person forces another to have sexual intercourse. Women and girls are usually the victims, although there are cases in which a homosexual rapes someone of the same sex. Most psychologists feel that rape is a crime of violence, that a rapist wants to hurt and frighten a woman rather than get sexual pleasure.

A woman who has been raped should go *immediately* to a hospital or a rape crisis center. A doctor will check her for injuries and will also look for sperm cells in the vagina, evidence that the rape happened. (No police report will be made without her consent. But if she delays or washes herself first, it may not be possible to prove anything.) The doctor also takes steps to prevent sexually transmitted disease.

The doctor can also recommend agencies that will provide free or inexpensive counseling. Victims need spiritual and emotional support as well as medical attention. A woman should seek help from her pastor or somebody she trusts as a committed Christian to receive the support in Christ that she needs.

How can a woman protect herself?

Many women believe that nothing can ever happen to them. They take chances that are foolish. But the best way to protect yourself is to stay away from dangerous situations, such as hitchhiking or walking alone at night. It's important to be alert so you will recognize danger when you see it. This true story illustrates why:

It was dusk when Karen and her friends got to the football game. They were hardly inside the gate when she decided she wanted the jacket she had left in the car. She hurried back to the parking lot, slipped on her jacket, and headed back to the stadium. "Hi, Karen!" called one of a little group of guys in the darker area next to the lot. "Come here a minute!" Karen was in the middle of the group before she realized she didn't know any of them. They must have heard her name when she first walked through the lot with her friends.

The biggest guy held a knife against Karen's ribs. Another grabbed her arm. They were walking her toward their car when another car distracted their attention. Karen wrenched her arm out of the guy's grasp and ran, leaving him holding her jacket. She never got the jacket back, and the young men were never caught, but she was safe!

What is incest?

Incest is having sexual relations with a member of your family or another close relative. It is a crime. Because of the prohibitions against incest, it is against the law to marry someone in one's immediate family—a brother or sister or father or mother. In many places first cousins are not allowed to marry.

Incest is more common than most people think. It happens in all kinds of families—rich and poor, white and black, churchgoing and nonreligious.

Usually, an older person will convince a younger or weaker person that this twisted form of sex is okay or that any guilt belongs to the younger person. This is a betrayal of trust and is never true. The victim is not guilty and will probably suffer severe spiritual and psychological damage if the relationship continues.

She (he) should firmly resist any future advances, and should talk over the problem with a parent or pastor or other trusted counselor. The victim of incest needs help. And so does the aggressor.

What is a prostitute?

A **prostitute** is a person who engages in sexual activity for money. Most prostitutes are women; most customers are men.

Both the number of prostitutes in the U.S. and Canada and the number of customers have dropped steadily in recent years. Because of pressure from churches and women's rights advocates, many police vice squads now arrest (and publicize names of) customers as well as the prostitutes themselves.

Why do promiscuous people act the way they do?

A **promiscuous** person has sexual intercourse with many different partners. Although a promiscuous woman is usually looked down on in our culture, a promiscuous man may be envied by some. However, researchers find very little difference in the personality and family backgrounds of these men and women. Their sex drive is no stronger than anyone else's, but they have a great need for something that will blot out their emotional problems.

Promiscuous people usually have very little self-confidence, accept little responsibility for their own behavior, and blame others for their own shortcomings. Because they do not take the time and effort to build a lasting relationship, they never discover how wonderful sex can be. Most sad of all, they are substituting sinful "thrills" for something much more thrilling: a close relationship with Jesus Christ.

Is a nymphomaniac a promiscuous woman?

Not exactly. A true **nymphomaniac** is a very sick woman. Her uncontrollable sexual desires cause her to seek sexual intercourse with anyone, at any cost. This mental illness is very rare.

Marriage counselors and psychologists report that most cases of alleged nymphomania turn out to be perfectly normal women. Sometimes husband and wife feel unable to talk to each other about their sexual relationship. The wife may be accused of being a nymphomaniac because at this time in her life she has a stronger sex drive than her husband does. Although they both are normal, they feel threatened because no woman wants to have sexual intercourse more than her husband does. Once the incorrect diagnosis is out of the way, the counselor is usually able to help them work things out.

What are sadism and masochism?

In both, sex is linked with violence, twisting God's good gift into something vile and nasty. Either physical or psychological pain is made part of the sex act. A **sadist** likes to give pain; a **masochist** either wants pain or is willing to suffer anything to please the partner.

People who believe that sex is shameful and dirty are most vulnerable to this mental disorder. Some psychologists blame an increase in the numbers of sadists and masochists on the common approval of aggressiveness and even violence in our society. For instance, movies and TV shows often glorify violence and combine it with sex.

What is fetishism?

Nearly everyone finds certain things more sexually exciting than others. We may be aroused by a particular part of the body (hair, breasts), by an article of clothing, or (if you can believe the ads) by a certain perfume. For a fetishist (usually male), this preference turns into a compulsion. One particular object, often a piece of clothing, becomes "the loved one" for him and takes the place of a sex partner in his life. He will steal or even hurt someone in order to get it.

Another form of fetishism is *kleptomania*, compulsive stealing. Here the sick person is usually a woman who feels unloved and unwanted. She steals objects that have no value to her, other than the sexual excitement she gets from the act of stealing and from the object itself.

In *pyromania*, the fetishist has a compulsive desire for fire. He gets sexual excitement from setting fires and watching them burn.

What is the difference between a transvestite and a transsexual? Are they homosexuals?

No. A **transvestite** is a person (usually male) who enjoys dressing in clothes of the opposite sex. Some habitually wear one item, like a bra or panties, under their own clothing. Others dress completely in women's clothing, either once in a while or—in extreme cases—all the time.

Most transvestites have normal sexual relationships with women. They marry and father children. They want only to be left alone to indulge in their desire to wear female clothing.

Transsexuals see themselves as the opposite sex; they feel trapped in the wrong body. They see the sex organs they were born with as deformities.

A typical transsexual is a man who wants to live the life of a woman. He wants a heterosexual relationship with another man but is not interested in homosexual men.

Some doctors now treat transsexuals with hormones. Sex change surgery is another option, now less common because too many operations were unsuccessful. Since either treatment is quite drastic, doctors study potential patients very carefully before accepting them. In spite of the number of transsexuals you may have seen on talk shows, this is a very rare condition.

What about homosexuality?

Homosexuals are people who are sexually attracted to those of their own sex. A homosexual man is sometimes called *gay*. A homosexual woman is called either gay or *lesbian*.

No one knows for sure why some people (about 2 out of every hundred) are homosexuals. Some experts believe homosexuality is an inborn characteristic. Others suggest that it is the result of sex hormones that are out of balance. Most homosexual people say that they didn't have a choice—that as they grew up they just "felt" homosexual. So the cause or causes of homosexuality are unknown.

What does the Bible say about homosexuality?

The Bible description of sexual love within marriage, "the two shall become one," clearly refers to a relationship between a man and a woman. Romans 1:27 says that homosexual behavior is one of the results of sinfulness. Nowhere in the Bible is there any approval for homosexuality as an alternate life-style.

While we as Christians cannot therefore condone homosexual behavior, we will want to show concern for the homosexual person. We will proclaim also to the homosexual that God forgives sin for Christ's sake and makes possible a new life through the power of the Holy Spirit.

Sometimes a boy or girl is labeled "homosexual" simply because of appearance and/or interests that may be different from the average. Such a wrongly applied label can follow a person for years and influence the way that person is treated by others. As Christians we surely will avoid name-calling, gossip, or labeling, which can seriously injure another person.

Can a person change from homosexuality to heterosexuality?

Some therapists have succeeded in helping people change from homosexual to heterosexual behavior. The therapy works only if the homosexual person has a strong desire to change.

How can I be sure I am not a homosexual?

Many young people worry unnecessarily about homosexual tendencies they suspect in themselves. They may have had one or more experiences with somebody of the same sex in which touching or other play resulted in orgasm. These experiences do not mean that someone is a homosexual.

It is also normal to have a deep attachment of friendship to someone of the same sex. David and Jonathan (1 Samuel 18), for instance, had a sincere love for each other that was very different from their normal sexual interest in the women they loved.

Many young people admire teachers or others who are the same sex. It is normal to admire someone very much and want to be near that person. Often this admiration helps you discover the direction you would like your own life to take.

No one should call himself (herself) homosexual until, as an adult, he (she) notices a constant, firm sexual interest in persons of the same sex. If you are worried about this, talk to your pastor or another adult about your feelings.

It often takes a long time for a young person to feel at ease with members of the other sex. Be patient with yourself. Remember that you are not the only one who fears rejection; others feel just as insecure as you do. Ask God to help you become more comfortable with your own sexuality. He will.

What about "safe sex," using a condom?

Medical studies show that condoms are not completely effective in preventing the sexual transmission of the HIV (AIDS) virus, although a latex condom used with spermicide containing non-axynol-9 is most effective. Studies also confirm that condoms do not offer total protection from chlamydia and human papilloma virus, two serious STDs that many sexually active teenagers have. The only real "safe sex" is with a lifelong marriage partner, with both partners remaining faithful to their marriage vows.

What about sexual harassment?

The law says that no one, man or woman, has to put up with "unwelcome sexual advances, requests for sexual favors, and other verbal or physical conduct of a sexual nature."

The sexual harassment law is aimed mostly at the workplace, but the courts have said that it also applies to schools when the behavior results "in an environment that causes a student fear, anxiety, shame, or embarrassment. It affects the student's ability to be in school."

Does that mean it's against the law for a man to flirt or kid with a woman?

Of course not. But you do have to be aware of the effect it's having on her. Is your flirting or kidding unwelcome? Did you continue kidding even after she let you know she didn't like it? Are you making school or work an uncomfortable place for her? If that kind of kidding around happens at a party rather than at school or work, it's probably not illegal—but it's still wrong.

My supervisor at work keeps asking me to take her out. I'm running out of excuses.

Tell her directly, "I like working with you but I don't want to date you." Don't make excuses; don't say anything that she might interpret as encouraging. If she persists, remind her that you've already said you are not interested and that sexual harassment is against the law. (Although most sexual harassment cases involve men who harass women, the law also applies to women who harass men.) If you are worried about losing your job, keep a diary describing exactly what happens between you.

What good will a diary do?

If you decide to tell the general manager what has been going on, your diary will be evidence that you are telling the truth. If you get angry at your supervisor for other reasons, you may be tempted to bring a sexual harassment charge against her to get her fired. Your diary will help you to keep to the exact truth of what happened—no more, no less.

What about the woman who leads a man on and then rejects him?

Both men and women need to be aware of the signals they are sending. What one sees as friendly teasing between buddies can be taken by the other as a come-on for a closer relationship. However, no mistaken signal can excuse the person who forces his attentions on another.

But what if a person gets so "hot" he can't stop himself?

That myth is popular among people who do not want to accept responsibility for their own actions. Controlling one's sexual drive is possible at any point from first arousal to orgasm.

I feel so powerless when guys at school make comments about my body and what they think I do with my boyfriend. How can I make them stop?

Tell them directly that you don't like what they are saying. It helps to say their names. "Kyle and Rick and Scott, when you talk that way to me, I feel so dirty and embarrassed that I don't even want to come to school. I want you to stop it now."

The guys probably tell themselves that you really like being teased, that you are secretly flattered by their attention. "You are wrong to think I enjoy that. It upsets me very much." Don't allow guys to tell you sexual jokes. Make it clear that you do not like their behavior. If they continue, tell them that their actions are against the law and you will bring formal charges against them if necessary.

I just couldn't talk back to them like that. Besides, I wonder if it would really help.

Polite, firm rejection of the harasser's behavior is a powerful strategy, but you do have other choices. If you can maintain a convincing poker face, you can ignore the harassment. Or you can ask for help from your friends, a friend of the boys, a teacher or counselor, or your parents.

A friend or classmate can be very effective in speaking up for a victim. Most harassers are people with very low self-esteem who try to build themselves up by putting others down. If they discover that others see their behavior as disgusting rather than funny, they will often stop. It takes courage to step in when someone is being harassed, but it's the right thing to do.

What's the big deal? Everybody gets kidded sometimes.

If it feels like harassment to the victim, it has gone beyond kidding. Sexual harassment often leaves people feeling very depressed, afraid, and unable to trust others. Many students report that they no longer want to come to school.

A nationwide survey of 1,632 high school students found that 85% of the girls and 76% of the boys reported being sexually harassed at school. Sexual comments, jokes, gestures, or looks were the most common form of harassment. 65% of the girls and 42% of the boys have also experienced unwelcome sexual touching, pinching, or grabbing.

What's meant by "date rape?"

Most rapes are committed by a trusted friend or **date** rather than by a stranger. The rapist may be a member of your church or the most popular person in the senior class.

Men need to understand the following:

- It is never okay to use force, coercion, alcohol, or drugs to pressure a woman into unwanted sexual contact. Such an act is a criminal offense.
- The amount of money you have spent on a woman entitles you to nothing.
- When a woman says no, no is what she means.
- If you enjoy violent movies, especially when the violence is directed at women, you may begin to think of violence as a way of dealing with problems and frustrations.
- No matter how aroused you get, you are able to control your sexual behavior.
- If alcohol and/or drugs have taken away your ability to think clearly and use good judgment, you are still responsible for your behavior.

Rape is a terrible sin. Although God forgives all sins, your victim's emotional and mental scars do not go away. Moreover, the victim may be forced to cope with an unwanted pregnancy, and the sad reality is that many in that situation choose abortion.

Women need to understand the following:

- Rape can happen to anyone.
- A popular, well-liked guy can be a rapist, especially if he's not used to taking no for an answer.
- A man whose words and/or actions show that he doesn't respect women is not someone you should trust.
- Submissive and docile women are natural victims. If you allow someone to impose his choices and decisions on you, you are sending a message you may regret.

The best protection against rape is to decide in advance what your sexual limits are and communicate them clearly and emphatically to your date. Don't expect him to guess what you are thinking. Make sure he has heard and understood you.

A rapist often begins with sexual harassment: unwanted touch, sexual jokes, comments with double meanings. He needs to hear a loud and clear message that you will leave immediately if this behavior continues.

If you feel uneasy about this man, get away! Trust your own feelings. Always arrange an alternate way to get home. Be sure you always have money with you.

If you use alcohol or drugs, you are much less likely to keep control of the situation. Watch out for the man who urges you to drink or experiment with drugs!

If he says or does something you don't like, tell him! Don't allow him to put the blame on you for "leading him on." He is responsible for his own actions.

If a man attempts to force himself on you, tell him that "after a woman says no, it's rape!" He must understand that this is criminal behavior, not just a guy who got carried away.

What is an "abusive relationship"?

Why does she stay with him? He treats her like dirt.

What does he see in her? He's been a different person ever since they started going together.

People often cling to a sick relationship because they see it as being better than being alone. When self-esteem gets low enough, it's easy to say, "This is all I deserve. If we break up, I'll never find anyone else who will love me." They forget that they are special people who are loved and valued by God. God can and will provide the courage to break free, the patience to endure a period of being alone, and the confidence needed to form a healthy relationship with someone new.

An abusive relationship is one in which there is a pattern of repeated verbal, emotional, and/or physical abuse by which one dating partner tries to control the other. A woman might threaten to break up with her male friend if he doesn't give up his other friends and outside interests and spend all his free time with her. A man might insist in making all the decisions and/or threaten violence if his female friend won't have sex with him.

Once a person gives in to any of these kinds of emotional blackmail, it becomes harder to stand up for his/her rights the next time. The abuser continues to do whatever it takes to make the dating partner toe the line.

If a woman allows a man to threaten violence or actually hurt her, that violence is likely to continue. There will be times when the abuser reforms and asks forgiveness, but he will almost always repeat the pattern of violence again and again. Only with outside help is he likely to accept responsibility for his own behavior and learn new ways of dealing with stress and conflict.

How can I tell when I'm in an abusive relationship?

Does your dating partner ...

- get angry easily and often?
- handle anger by destroying things or treating people roughly?
- constantly put you down?
- frequently embarrass you in front of your friends?
- refuse to believe he/she has really hurt you?
- brag about previous girlfriends/boyfriends?
- insist on making all the decisions that affect both of you?
- try to stop you from ordinary socializing with friends, visiting your family, or talking with the other sex?
- use threats to make you do what he/she wants? (I'll leave you; I'll tell everyone your secret; I'll hit you again; I'll kill myself.)
- make you feel you deserve to be punished or abused?
- isolate you from people who really care about you?
- get so upset when you express a different opinion that you always give in, just to keep peace?

If you said yes to even one of the above questions, you are in an abusive relationship and need to get help. If you do nothing, things will almost surely get worse. Don't even think about marrying a person who treats you badly. You deserve to have a relationship of equality and love, not one of dependence and fear.

Chapter 10

Scrapbook

This chapter is a scrapbook: a collection of quotes, prayers and thought-starters. We hope you'll use them as ways to begin talking with God about your sexuality, and as reminders that you are not—and never will be—alone.

Not Good Enough

Fear not, for I have redeemed you. I have summoned you by name; you are mine (Isaiah 43:1).

The truth is, I'm a failure. Not good enough to get on the team—to have dates—to be popular—to make my parents proud of me.

Big feet. Knobby knees. A million pimples. Hair that won't act like I want it to.

Why, Lord? Why do I always say such dumb things—if I can think of anything to say at all? Why do people ignore me, act like I'm not even there? Why am I always on the outside, watching other people have fun?

I know it's my own fault sometimes. I get so discouraged I give up before I even start. Some days I hardly speak to anyone. Other times, something inside me makes me act stupid and silly—to get their attention, I guess.

Keep telling me I am Yours, Lord Jesus. Remind me—again and again—that You love me just as I am. Since I don't like myself very much, show me how I can change. Give me opportunities to make friends. Help me appreciate the specialness You have created within me. Help me to listen when You call my name.

Too Far, Too Soon

For what I do is not the good I want to do; no, the evil I do not want to do—this I keep on doing ... The mind of sinful man is death, but the mind controlled by the Spirit is life and peace (Romans 7:19; 8:6).

What happens to my good intentions when I'm with her? Why does my desire for her override everything else? Because I am so much in love with her, I forget plans for the future—parents' love for me—my own deep knowledge of right and wrong.

At least I *think* I'm in love. When we are together, I always want to be close to her. She's the kindest, most fun, prettiest girl I've ever met. Being with her is wonderful. Is that love? Will I still feel the same way five years from now?

I wonder how she feels about our growing closer together. What does she really want? I know we shouldn't go on like this, but what will she think if I back off now? Maybe we should talk over what our limits ought to be—but I wouldn't know how to begin.

God, thank You for my sexuality, for the body you have given me. But I need more! For one thing, I need Your forgiveness for so often misusing Your gifts. I need Your support, Your wisdom as I turn around and begin again. Give me the right words to talk to her about how we feel about each other.

Lord Jesus, I really do want Your Spirit to control my life. Help me remember that tonight!

In Love, I Think

Shout for joy to the LORD, all the earth, burst into jubilant song with music; make music to the LORD with the harp, with the harp and the sound of singing, with trumpets and the blast of the ram's horn—shout for joy before the LORD, the King (Psalm 98:4–6).

I feel like cartwheels across the lawn, like fizzy bubbles rising to the top of a glass of ginger ale, like trumpets and cymbals and drums.

I think—I am almost positive!—that he likes me as much as I like him. Surely two people couldn't laugh and talk and enjoy life together as we do, without both realizing that something special is happening. It's hard to believe that a few weeks ago we hardly knew each other.

So far, we haven't spoken much about serious things—yet somehow I know You mean as much to him as You do to me. The way he treats me—and the way he treats others—tells me a lot. When I see him at church, I feel sure he is there by choice.

Lord, what is this wonderful feeling? When I'm near him, my bones melt. My heart pounds. I feel dizzy. Is this truly love, or just the excitement of getting to know someone who really attracts me? Whatever it is, it's the most thrilling thing that has ever happened to me, and I don't want it to ever end.

Yes, Lord. I know You have a plan for me, much better than anything I could work out by myself. Maybe he is part of Your plan—or maybe this love (?) I feel now is only for today.

Whatever happens in the future, I feel great today. The happy feeling inside me right now has to be a gift from You—thank You! Thank You, Lord Jesus, for caring about my todays and about my future. Because I am important to You, I can enjoy today, and still learn and plan and think and grow. I can leave my future in Your loving hands.

 Decisions

We live by faith, not by sight (2 Corinthians 5:7).

Ever since I can remember, I have longed to be grown up. It's fun to think about having my own car—being able to stay out as long as I want—being free to travel and work and play at a pace I set. The really hard choices—about love and marriage and children—have seemed very remote and far away.

But lately I've met people not much older than I who have already made their choices. At 16 or 17 they have found themselves in situations that will affect the rest of their lives. How do I know I won't be trapped by my own mistakes?

Sometimes I think being alone is the only way to keep from being hurt. I see steady couples torn by jealousy and hurt feelings, marriages ripped apart, families who do nothing but yell at each other. Is love really worth the risk?

You think so, don't You, Jesus? You allowed Yourself to be tortured, deserted by friends, misunderstood—for love's sake. You were willing to suffer anything to make the church—all of us—your bride. I know I can always count on Your love for me, on Your unchanging presence in my life. Troubles may come, but I cling to the belief that You will show me how to love and be loved.

Although I have made many mistakes, You have taught me how to choose friends and how to be a friend. Guide me now as I learn how to be a loving person.

Not Far Enough?

For this reason He had to be made like His brothers in every way ... Because He Himself suffered when He was tempted, He is able to help those who are being tempted (Hebrews 2:17–18).

Is there something wrong with me? Am I incomplete, Lord? Unmasculine? What do other people say about me behind my back? Do they call me cold? Or stupid?

Does everyone else really do it? Is it as great as they claim? Am I missing something wonderful by waiting? Lord, when they joke about the girls they've been with, I don't know what to say. Usually I pretend not to understand their questions—or I kid around with them, say something they can take any way they like. Either way, I feel like a fool.

I like girls, Lord. I'm pretty sure that my sex drive is as strong as anybody's. And even though I'm careful not to let things go too far, I *want* to be free and warm and loving. And sometimes I feel very unwilling to wait any longer. I want it *now*.

What kinds of feelings did You experience, Jesus, as You were growing up? I have trouble picturing You struggling with problems and temptations like mine—yet I know You were like me in this way as in all others.

Help me, Lord, to remember You understand how I feel, so I can talk and question and confess freely to You— and get Your power to act in Your way.

GLOSSARY

Abortion (a-BOR-shun) The premature termination of a pregnancy. There are three types:

Voluntary, a procedure performed at the request of the pregnant woman.

Spontaneous, a natural termination usually due to some abnormal development of the fetus.

Therapeutic, a medically recommended procedure prompted by abnormal developments that threaten the mother's life or the fetus.

Abstinence (AB-stin-ens) To voluntarily avoid. In sexual connotation, to refrain from sexual intercourse.

Adolescence (ad-uh-LES-sens) The period of life between puberty and adulthood.

Adultery (a-DULL-ter-ee) Sexual intercourse with a person who is legally married to someone else. The term is often used to describe any sexual intercourse outside of marriage.

AIDS (Acquired Immune Deficiency Syndrome) A life-threatening viral disease most commonly transmitted through exchange of blood and/or semen either by sexual contact or by use of dirty needles in "shooting" drugs.

Amniocentesis (am-nee-o-sen-TEE-sis) A procedure whereby a sample of the amniotic fluid surrounding the fetus is drawn and analyzed to detect possible birth defects.

Amnion (AM-nee-on) The thin membrane that forms the sac of water surrounding the fetus within the uterus. Contains amniotic fluid, in which the fetus is immersed for protection against shocks and jolts.

Androgen (AN-dro-jen) A hormone that influences growth and the sex drive in the male. Produces masculine secondary sex characteristics (voice changes, hair growth, etc.).

Anus (AY-nuss) The opening at the base of the buttocks through which solid waste is eliminated from the intestines

Artificial Insemination The medical procedure of injecting semen into the vagina close to the cervix by artificial means; can enable pregnancy in spite of fertility problems.

AZT A drug that, for some people, slows the development of AIDS.

Birth Control See Contraception.

Bisexual (by-SECKS-shoo-al) Having both male and female sex organs. Commonly-used term to describe a sexual interest in both sexes.

Bladder (BLAD-er) A sac in the pelvic region where urine is stored until elimination.

Breech Birth The birth position when the baby's feet or buttocks appear first instead of the usual (headfirst) position.

Caesarean Section (si-SAIR-ee-an) (Caesarean Birth; "C" Section) Delivery of a baby by surgical incision through the abdomen into the uterus.

Castration (kas-TRAY-shun) Removal of the sex glands—the testicles in men, the ovaries in women.

Cervix (SER-viks) The narrow, lower part of the uterus, which opens into the deep portion of the vagina.

Chancre (SHANG-ker) A small sore or ulcerated area, usually on the genitals, which is the first symptom of syphilis.

Change of Life See Climacteric; Menopause.

Chastity (CHAS-ti-tee) Abstention from illicit sexual intercourse.

Chlamydia (kla-MID-ee-ah) See Sexually Transmitted Disease.

Chromosome (KRO-mo-soam) One of the more or less rodlike bodies found in the nucleus of all cells, containing the heredity factors or genes. 22 pairs of chromosomes account for a person's hereditary characteristics. The 23d pair determines sex. See X Chromosome and Y Chromosome.

Circumcision (ser-kum-SIZH-un) Surgical removal of the foreskin or prepuce of the penis. Originally a Jewish rite performed as a sign of reception into their faith; now generally performed for purposes of cleanliness.

Climacteric (kly-MACK-ter-ik) The time of physical and emotional change—the end of menstruation in women and a lessening of sex-hormone production in both sexes. See Menopause and Midlife Crisis.

Climax See Orgasm.

Clitoris (KLIT-or-is) A small, highly sensitive female organ located just above the urethra. Compares to the penis in males.

Coitus (KO-i-tus) (Copulation) Sexual intercourse between male and female, in which the penis is inserted into the vagina.

Conception (kon-SEP-shun) (Impregnation) Penetration of the ovum (female egg cell) by a sperm, resulting in development of an embryo—new life.

Condom See Contraception.

Congenital (kon-JEN-i-tal) A condition existing from birth. May or may not be inherited.

Contraception (kon-trah-SEP-shun) (Birth control) The prevention of conception by use of devices, drugs, or other means in sexual intercourse. Commonly used methods:

Birth Control Pill A contraceptive drug made of synthetic hormones that prevent ovulation and sometimes the implanting of a fertilized egg. Available only by prescription and must be taken as prescribed.

Condom (KON-dum) A device made of thin rubber that prevents sperm from entering the vagina. Male: a thin rubber sheath placed over the penis. Female: a polyurethane sheath that fits inside the vagina. The open end of the sheath covers the vulva.

Vaginal Foam, Jelly, Suppositories, etc. Non-prescription products for the female that are applied within the vagina. Most contain a spermicide—a chemical substance that destroys sperm cells.

Diaphragm (DIE-a-fram) A thin rubber disc that covers the cervix and prevents sperm from entering the uterus. Must be individually fitted by a doctor.

Premature Withdrawal Withdrawal of the penis from the vagina before ejaculation. Largely unreliable because of possible release of sperm before ejaculation.

Rhythm Method Abstinence from intercourse during the woman's fertile days as determined by her menstrual cycle.

Cowper's glands Small glands lying alongside the male urethra which secrete part of the seminal fluid.

Cunnilingus (kun-i-LING-us) The act of applying the mouth or tongue to the vulva, to stimulate the female.

D&C (Dilatation & Curettage) A medical procedure in which the cervix is dilated and a spoon-shaped medical instrument called a curette is used to scrape the lining of the uterus.

Delivery The process of giving birth.

Douche (doosh) The cleansing of the vagina with a stream of liquid solution or water.

Ejaculation (ee-jack-yoo-LAY-shun) The discharge of semen from the penis.

Embryo (EM-bree-oh) The unborn in its earliest stages of development. In humans, the fertilized ovum during the first eight weeks of its growth.

Endometrium (en-doh-MEE-tree-um) The lining of the uterus, which thickens and fills with blood in preparation for a fertilized ovum.

Epididymis (ep-ah-DID-i-miss) The mass of tiny coils connecting the testicles with the sperm duct.

Erection (ee-RECK-shun) The enlargement and hardening of the penis or clitoris as tissues fill with blood, usually during sexual excitement.

Erogenous Zone (i-RAH-jen-us) Any area of the body that is sexually sensitive or stimulating such as mouth, lips, breasts, nipples, and genitals.

Erotic (ee-RAH-tik) Sexually stimulating.

Estrogen (ESS-tro-jen) A hormone that affects functioning of the menstrual cycle and produces female secondary sex characteristics (breast development, widened hips, etc.).

Eunuch (YOO-nuck) A castrated male.

Exhibitionist (ex-i-BISH-un-ist) A person who compulsively exposes his/her sex organs in public.

Extramarital (ex-tra-MARE-i-tal) "Outside of marriage"; often used to refer to illicit sexual intercourse, i.e., "extramarital affair."

Fallopian Tube (fa-LOW-pee-an) The tube through which the egg passes from each ovary to the uterus.

Fellatio (fel-LAY-show) The act of applying the mouth or tongue to the penis to stimulate the male.

Fertility The ability to reproduce.

Fertilization Penetration of the female ovum by a single sperm, resulting in conception.

Fetus (FEE-tuss) The unborn child from the third month after conception until birth.

Foreplay The beginning stage of sexual intercourse, during which partners may kiss, caress, and touch each other in order to achieve full sexual arousal.

Foreskin The loose skin covering the tip of the penis, removed during circumcision. Also called the prepuce (PREE-pus).

Fornication (for-ni-KAY-shun) Sexual intercourse between unmarried men and women.

Frigidity (fri-JID-i-tee) Commonly used term for the sexual dysfunction in which a woman is unable to respond to sexual stimulation.

Gene (jean) The carrier for hereditary traits in chromosomes.

Genital Herpes See Sexually Transmitted Disease.

Genitalia (jen-i-TAIL-ya) (Genitals; Genital Organs) Visible reproductive or sex organs. Usually denotes vagina, vulva, and clitoris in females and the penis and testicles in males.

Gestation (jes-TAY-shun) The period from conception to birth, approximately nine months.

Glans (glanz) The head of the penis exposed when the foreskin is pushed back, or after circumcision.

Gonorrhea (gon-er-EE-uh) See Sexually Transmitted Disease.

Gynecologist (guy-na-KOLL-o-jist) A physician who specializes in the treatment of female sexual and reproductive organs.

Heredity (her-ED-it-ee) Traits, characteristics, or diseases transmitted from parents to children.

Hermaphrodite (her-MAF-ro-dite) An individual born with both male and female sex organs.

Heterosexual (het-er-o-SECK-shoo-al) One who is sexually attracted to or sexually active with persons of the other sex.

HIV (Human Immunodeficiency Virus) The virus that causes AIDS.

Homosexual (ho-mo-SECK-shoo-al) One who is sexually attracted to or sexually active with persons of one's own sex.

Hormone (HOR-moan) A chemical substance, produced by an endocrine gland, that has a particular effect on the function of other organs in the body.

Human Papilloma Virus (HPV) Infection (pap-il-LO-ma) See Sexually Transmitted Disease.

Hymen (HIGH-men) A thin membrane that partially closes the entrance to the vagina. Sometimes called the maidenhead.

Hysterectomy (hiss-ter-ECK-toh-mee) Surgical removal of the uterus. May include removal of one or both ovaries (oophorectomy).

Impotence (IM-po-tens) A type of male sexual dysfunction; inability to achieve or maintain erection of the penis during sexual intercourse.

Incest (IN-sest) Sexual intercourse between close relatives such as father and daughter, mother and son, or brother and sister.

Intercourse, Sexual See Coitus.

Jock Itch A fungus infection causing skin irritation in the genital area.

Labor The birth stage in which the cervix gradually dilates, allowing strong contractions of the uterine muscles to push the baby through the vagina and out of the mother's body.

Lactation (lak-TAY-shun) The production and secretion of milk by the mammary glands in the mother's breasts, following childbirth. The process continues as long as she nurses her child.

Lesbian (LEZ-be-an) A female homosexual.

Libido (li-BEE-doe) See Sex Drive.

Maidenhead See Hymen.

Masochism (MASS-o-kizm) Cruelty to self; receiving sexual pleasure from having pain inflicted or by being harshly dominated.

Masturbation (mass-ter-BAY-shun) Self-stimulation of one's sex organs, often to the point of orgasm.

Menarche (me-NAR-kee) The onset of the menstrual cycle in a girl.

Menopause (MEN-o-pawz) (Change of Life; Climacteric) The end of menstruation in women, usually between the ages of 45 and 55.

Menstruation (men-stroo-AY-shun) The discharge through the vagina of blood from the uterus. This menstrual "period" usually occurs every 28-30 days in females, between puberty and menopause.

Midlife Crisis Current term for the change of life (climacteric) in men, usually between ages 50 and 60; sometimes called male menopause. May evoke feelings of restlessness and failure.

Miscarriage The natural expulsion of the fetus from the uterus before it is mature enough to survive, usually due to some abnormal development.

Nocturnal Emission (nok-TER-nal ee-MISH-un) (Wet Dream) Involuntary male erection and ejaculation during sleep.

Nymphomaniac (nim-foe-MAY-nee-ack) A female who experiences excessive sexual desire.

Obstetrician (ob-ste-TRISH-un) A physician who specializes in the care of women during pregnancy, childbirth, and immediately thereafter.

Oral Sex See Cunnilingus; Fellatio.

Orgasm (OR-gazm) (Climax) The peak of excitement in sexual activity.

Ovaries (OH-va-rees) The two female sex glands found on either side of the uterus, in which the ova (egg cells) are formed. They also produce hormones that influence female body characteristics.

Ovulation (ah-vyoo-LAY-shun) Release of the mature (ripe) ovum from the ovary to the fallopian tube.

Ovum (OH-vum) (Plural: ova) Female reproductive cell (egg) found in the ovary. After fertilization by a male sperm, the human egg develops into an embryo and then a fetus.

Penis (PEE-nis) Male sex organ through which semen is discharged and urine is passed.

Pituitary (pih-TOO-it-air-ee) A gland at the base of the brain that controls functions of all the other ductless glands, especially sex glands, adrenals, and thyroid.

Placenta (pluh-SEN-ta) The sponge like organ that connects the fetus to the lining of the uterus by means of the umbilical cord. It serves to feed the fetus and to dispose of waste. Expelled from the uterus after the birth of a child (afterbirth).

Pornography (por-NOG-raf-ee) Literature, motion pictures, art, or other means of expression that, without any concern for personal or moral values, intend simply to be sexually arousing.

Pregnancy (PREG-nan-see) Period from conception to birth; the condition of having a developing embryo or fetus within the female body.

Prenatal (pree-NAY-tal) Before birth.

Progesterone (pro-JES-te-roan) (Progestin) The female "pregnancy hormone" that prepares the uterus to receive the fertilized ovum.

Promiscuous (pro-MISS-kyoo-us) Engaging in sexual intercourse with many persons; engaging in casual sexual relationships.

Prostate (PRAH-state) Male gland that surrounds the urethra and neck of the bladder and secretes part of the seminal fluid.

Prostitute (PRAH-sti-toot) An individual who engages in sexual activity for money.

Puberty (PYOO-ber-tee) The period of rapid development that marks the end of childhood; sex organs mature and produce either ovaries or sperm; the girl becomes a young woman and the boy a young man.

Pubic (PYOO-bik) Regarding the lower part of the abdominal area, where hair grows in a triangular patch.

Rape (rayp) Forcible sexual intercourse with a person who does not consent.

Rectum (RECK-tum) The lower end of the large intestine, ending at the anus.

Rhythm Method See Contraception.

Sadism (SADE-izm) Cruelty; receiving sexual pleasure by inflicting pain on the sexual partner.

Safe Period The interval in the menstrual cycle when the female is presumably not ovulating and therefore unable to become pregnant.

Safe Sex The claim that using a condom will prevent STDs. Much medical research disproves the claim. The only truly safe sex is to remain a virgin until married, and then have intercourse only with an uninfected spouse.

Scrotum (SKRO-tum) The sac of skin suspended between the male's legs that contains the testicles.

Semen (SEE-men) (Seminal Fluid; Seminal Emission) The fluid made up of sperm, secretions from the seminal vesicles, prostate and Cowper's glands, and the epididymis. Ejaculated through the penis when the male reaches orgasm.

Seminal Vesicles (SEM-i-nal VESS-i-cals) Two storage pouches for sperm (which is produced in the testicles). Located on either side of the prostate, they are attached to and open into the sperm ducts.

Sex Drive (Libido) The desire for sexual activity.

Sex, Oral See Cunnilingus; Fellatio.

Sex Organs Commonly refers to the male penis and female vagina.

Sexual Dysfunction Term used to describe problems in sexual performance.

Sexual Intercourse See Coitus.

Sexually Transmitted Disease (STD) Any of a variety of contagious diseases contracted almost entirely by sexual intercourse. Some of the most common are AIDS, chlamydia, genital herpes, gonorrhea, human papilloma virus (HPV) disease, trichomoniasis, and syphilis.

Smegma (SMEG-mah) A thick accumulation of secretions under the foreskin of the penis or around the clitoris, which has an unpleasant odor.

Sodomy (SAH-dah-mee) Any of a variety of sexual behaviors, broadly defined by law as deviant, such as sexual intercourse by humans with animals, mouth-genital contact, or anal intercourse between human beings.

Sperm The male reproductive cell(s), produced in the testicles, having the capacity to fertilize the female ova, resulting in pregnancy.

Spermatic Duct (sper-MAT-ik dukt) (Vas Deferens) The tube in the male through which sperm passes from the epididymis to the seminal vesicles and urethra.

Spermatic Cord The tube in the male by which the testicle is suspended; contains the sperm ducts, veins, and nerves.

Spermicide See Contraception.

Spontaneous Abortion See Miscarriage.

Sterility (ster-ILL-it-ee) The inability to reproduce.

Sterilization (ster-ill-ih-ZAY-shun) A procedure by which a male or female is rendered unable to produce children, but can still engage in sexual intercourse. Some of the most common surgical methods:

Laparoscopy (la-pa-ROS-ko-pee) Tiny incisions in the abdomen, through which the fallopian tubes are cut or cauterized. Also called "Band-Aid Sterilization."

Tubal Ligation (TOO-bul lie-GAY-shun) The surgeon cuts and ties the ends of both fallopian tubes after making a larger incision in the abdomen or by going through the vagina.

Vasectomy (vas-ECK-toe-mee) The male sperm-carrying duct is cut, part is removed, and the ends tied.

Syphilis See Sexually Transmitted Disease.

Testicles (TESS-ti-klz) (Testes) The two male sex glands that produce sperm suspended within a sac of skin between the legs.

Testosterone (tes-TOSS-ter-own) Male sex hormone produced by the testes; causes and maintains male secondary sex characteristics (voice change, hair growth, etc.).

Transsexual (trans-SECK-shoo-al) One who feels psychologically like a member of the other sex and is willing to undergo "sex change" surgery to achieve the outward appearance of the other sex.

Transvestite One who has a compulsion to dress in the clothing of the other sex.

Trichomoniasis (trick-uh-muh-NY-uh-sis) See Sexually Transmitted Disease.

Umbilical Cord (um-BILL-i-kal) The cord connecting the fetus to the placenta, through which the fetus receives nourishment.

Urethra (yoo-REE-thra) The duct through which urine passes from the bladder and is eliminated from the body.

Urologist (yoo-RAHL-i-jist) A physician who specializes in treating urinary tract problems of both sexes, as well as the genital tract of males.

Uterus (YOO-ter-us)   The small, muscular, pear-shaped female organ in which the fetus develops; has the ability to accommodate the growing child (children).

Vagina (vuh-JY-na) (Birth Canal) The canal in the female body between the uterus and the vulva; receives the penis during intercourse; the canal through which an infant passes at birth.

Vas Deferens (VAS DEF-er-enz) See Spermatic Duct.

Vasectomy See Sterilization.

Virgin (VER-jin) A person who has never had sexual intercourse.

Vulva (VUL-va) The female's external sex organs, including the Labia majora and Labia minora, the outer and inner folds of skin (lips) surrounding the vagina, and the clitoris.

Wasserman Test A blood test to determine present or past infection with syphilis.

Wet Dream See Nocturnal Emission.

Womb (WOOM) See Uterus.

X Chromosome A chromosome that determines sex, present in all female ova and in one-half of a male's sperm. If the egg is fertilized by a sperm having an X chromosome, a female will be conceived (XX).

Y Chromosome A sex-determining chromosome present in one-half of a male's sperm. If an ovum is fertilized by a sperm with a Y chromosome, a male will be conceived (XY).